T0328476

Cambridge Elements ≡

Elements in Economics of European Integration
edited by
Nauro F. Campos
University College London

THE ROAD TO MONETARY UNION

Richard Pomfret

University of Adelaide

CAMBRIDGE
UNIVERSITY PRESS

CAMBRIDGE
UNIVERSITY PRESS

University Printing House, Cambridge CB2 8BS, United Kingdom

One Liberty Plaza, 20th Floor, New York, NY 10006, USA

477 Williamstown Road, Port Melbourne, VIC 3207, Australia

314–321, 3rd Floor, Plot 3, Splendor Forum, Jasola District Centre, New Delhi – 110025, India

79 Anson Road, #06–04/06, Singapore 079906

Cambridge University Press is part of the University of Cambridge.

It furthers the University's mission by disseminating knowledge in the pursuit of education, learning, and research at the highest international levels of excellence.

www.cambridge.org
Information on this title: www.cambridge.org/9781108965477
DOI: 10.1017/9781108962315

First published 2021

A catalogue record for this publication is available from the British Library.

ISBN 978-1-108-96547-7 Paperback
ISSN 2634-0763 (online)
ISSN 2634-0755 (print)

The Road to Monetary Union

Elements in Economics of European Integration

DOI: 10.1017/9781108962315
First published online: February 2021

Richard Pomfret
University of Adelaide

Author for correspondence: Richard Pomfret, richard.pomfret@adelaide.edu.au

Abstract: The Road to Monetary Union analyzes, in non-technical language, the process leading to adoption of a common currency for the European Union. The monetary union process involved different issues at different times and the contemporary global background mattered. The Element explains why monetary union was attempted and failed in the 1970s, and why the process was restarted in 1979, accelerated after 1992 and completed for a core group of EU members in 1999. It asks why euro membership expanded in the 2000s, but still does not include all EU members. It analyzes connections between eurozone membership and Greece's sovereign debt crisis. It concludes with analysis of how the eurozone works today and with discussion of its prospects for the 2020s. The approach is primarily economic, while acknowledging the role of politics (timing) and history (path dependence). A theme is to challenge simplistic ideas (e.g. that the euro has failed) with fuller analysis of competing pressures to shape the nature of monetary union.

Keywords: monetary union, Eurozone, European Union

ISBNs: 9781108965477 (PB), 9781108962315 (OC)
ISSNs: 2634-0763 (online), 2634-0755 (print)

Contents

Preface   v

1 Introduction   1

2 Theories   3

3 The Werner Report and the Snake   9

4 The European Monetary System   12

5 The Maastricht Treaty and Creation of the Euro   17

6 The Euro Expanding   23

7 The Sovereign Debt Crisis and its Aftermath   28

8 Conclusions   41

Abbreviations   45

References   46

Preface

Monetary union has been one of the most dramatic components of European economic integration. It was attempted by the then-nine members of the European Economic Community in the 1970s and failed dismally. The project was relaunched in the 1980s and 1990s. The euro was introduced for financial transactions in 1999 and on 1 January 2002 euro bank notes became the common currency in twelve EU member countries. By January 2020, nineteen EU members were using the euro.

Monetary union among such a large and varied group of independent countries was unprecedented. Economists could easily explain the failure of the 1970s and many predicted in the 1990s that monetary union would not happen and, if it did happen, it would not last. By 2020, both predictions had been disproven, although many critics continue to predict the currency's doom.

This contribution to the **Cambridge Elements: Economics of European Integration** series describes and analyzes the road to monetary union. It is essentially an economics story with steps along the road being accelerated or delayed by political developments. European monetary union is a unique story because it is associated with a unique process of deep integration among independent countries.

Fixed exchange rates among independent countries – and the extreme case of currency union – are difficult because they involve acceptance of either restrictions on capital mobility or on monetary policy. Small open economies such as Luxembourg may join a currency union because they have little monetary policy independence anyway, but larger economies will be more cautious. In the early stages of European integration, the large member countries were unwilling to accept these restrictions, especially in the unstable global economic conditions of the 1970s when the large European countries had differing monetary policy priorities. By the 1990s, following creation of the Single Market and general agreement that moderating inflation should be the principal target of monetary policy, most of the EU member countries were willing to accept the need for a common currency. This story is told in Sections 3–6.

The last two sections consider the operation and future of the eurozone. After a relatively calm first decade, the eurozone faced a major shock as several members experienced sovereign debt crises, of which Greece's was the most challenging. The crises raised the fundamental question of the extent to which financial crises in a common currency area were national or eurozone-wide problems. If all members are required to help in resolving a debt crisis, what are the implications for common policies towards the financial system?

A second systemic issue concerns the relationship between the EU members in the eurozone and those members not using the common currency. To what extent will financial and economic policies, and their ramifications, be determined by the former group, leaving the non-users as a second-class periphery outside mainstream EU policy discussions? Following Brexit in January 2020, the balance between euro and non-euro countries within the EU has shifted dramatically: of the 446 million people in the EU27, 341 million live in the eurozone and 105 million outside the eurozone.

* * *

Material in this Element is related to sections of my book on European Economic Integration (Harvard University Press, forthcoming), which provides deeper analysis of the broader economic integration process in Europe. The Element was written while I held the Jean Monnet Chair in the Economics of European Integration (2017–20), co-funded by the European Union and the University of Adelaide.

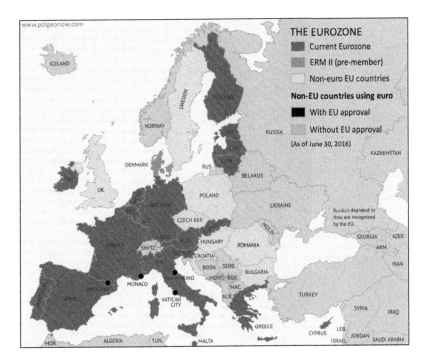

Map Countries using the Euro, January 2020
Source: www.polgeonow.com/2014/08/map-which-countries-use-euro-plus-this.html
(accessed 11 January 2020), covered by Creative Commons license https://creativecom
mons.org/licenses/by-sa/3.0/legalcode

1 Introduction

Monetary union has been one of the most controversial and paradoxical elements of European integration. It is paradoxical because, despite many predictions that a common currency would never be created and, if it did happen, it was bound to collapse, monetary union has happened and two decades later the common currency still exists.[1] In contrast to the doomsday scenario, the road to monetary union can be presented as a drawn-out odyssey from initial steps to establishment of a single currency over the last three decades of the twentieth century. The reality is more complex than a simple story of overcoming obstacles to achieve the happy ending and many pessimists still believe that the story is a tragedy.[2]

The aim of this Element is to provide an analysis of the road to monetary union with explanations of why the pessimists were confounded by the commitment to establish a common currency and why that currency has survived a tumultuous decade in the 2010s. It will end with a cautious review of the euro's prospects in the 2020s.

The analysis combines economics, politics and history. The underlying theme is that economics is the long-run driver; as the EU moves towards deeper integration and more common policies, the costs of monetary disunion increase. However, the process has not been steady. Politics often determined the timing of the next step (e.g. French pressure on the German Chancellor to think of Europe as Germany reunified in 1990), but it has not determined the direction of change. This view is in opposition to the characterization of the euro by Thomas Mayer (2012, 1): 'a highly ambitious political project pursued with an occasional reckless negligence of economics'. The historical background has influenced timing (e.g. the collapse of the Bretton Woods system and the first oil shock ensured the rapid destruction of the Snake in the 1970s), while the calmer global economic situation for almost a decade after the introduction of the euro in 1999 helped the establishment of the new currency. Some personalities stand out in more traditional accounts of European economic and monetary union; the policymakers and influencers are mentioned in my account, but the impersonal economic forces were stronger and, for example, heads of the Commission who were influential along the road to monetary union (e.g. Roy Jenkins in 1977/8 or

---

[1] Feldstein (1992) was probably the most influential. Jonung and Drea (2009) provide an exhaustive survey of US economists' predictions.

[2] For example, the publisher's publicity flyer to the updated 2020 paperback edition tells us that Ashoka Mody's book *Euro Tragedy: A Drama in Nine Acts* 'makes clear that the euro's structural flaws will continue to haunt the continent'. The title of the 2016 book by Nobel Laureate Joseph Stiglitz, *The Euro: How a Common Currency Threatens the Future of Europe*, describes the content and conclusion.

Jacques Delors in 1988/9) were pushing the accelerator rather than changing direction.

* * *

The next section reviews three branches of international economics that are relevant to analyzing currency union. Optimum currency area theory has been the most commonly applied theoretical framework. It is useful in highlighting economic costs and benefits of adopting a common currency, but less successful in explaining when a specific currency union is formed or dissolved. A more empirical strand of the literature measures the impact of a common currency on bilateral trade. Finally, the phenomenon of global value chains in which trade occurs at more fragmented levels of specialization has reflected the increased importance of trade facilitation, of which a common currency may be part. The significance of the last two topics is that the benefits of currency union may change over time.

The following five sections focus on different stages along the road to European monetary union. The first step, introduced in the 1970s, was an abject failure which quickly broke down as the large economies withdrew their currencies from the process in a classic example of the Impossible Trinity: a fixed exchange rate, capital mobility and an independent monetary policy cannot co-exist. Governments abandoned the fixed exchange rate system intended as a preliminary to monetary union rather than lose monetary policy independence.

Within a few years, however, European leaders attempted to revive the process, and with more success. This cannot be explained in an optimum currency area framework. Better explanations are that the European leaders recognized the benefits of constant exchange rates in reducing the costs of private and public transactions and were converging on agreed-upon monetary policies that prioritized low inflation. On several occasions, countries had to decide between fixed exchange rates and monetary policy independence, most notably following the 1990 reunification of Germany and the subsequent rise in German interest rates. Section 5 describes how the 1992 currency crisis provided the final push to change fixed exchange rates into a common currency for most of the European Union member countries.

The monetary union was successful in its first decade as inflation remained low in the 2000s and more countries adopted the euro (Section 6). However, low interest rate differentials, as lenders believed without exchange rate risk all eurozone public debt was equally safe, encouraged excessive borrowing by some countries. In 2009, Greece announced that it was unable to maintain its debt-servicing obligations.

The Greek crisis that dominated much of the decade of the 2010s is the most controversial part of the road to monetary union (Section 7). Should Greece have been allowed into the eurozone? How could Greece's mounting debt have been better monitored? Could the conditional financial assistance to Greece have been better managed? Should Greece have left the eurozone and devalued its currency? These questions are difficult to answer because it is hard to specify the counterfactual situation. Many critics argue that the eurozone was introduced too soon, without institutions that may have fore-stalled the Greek crisis. Many of these institutions were being introduced as the crisis was playing out, which says something about policymaking in crisis periods.

The final section draws conclusions.

2 Theories

A difficulty for evaluating monetary integration has been the absence of a suitable theoretical model. Since the 1960s, optimum currency area (OCA) theory has been a common approach and it remains the foundation for many textbook analyses of European monetary integration. The OCA literature is helpful in highlighting the trade-offs associated with changing currency domains, but it is less useful in explaining the size of actual currency zones or the magnitude of the costs and benefits from currency unification.

A more recent literature has addressed the impact of currency union on trade. While the econometric evidence confirms the presumed positive sign of the relationship, there has been debate over the size of the impact. The very large effect estimated in the pioneering paper by Rose (2000) attracted considerable attention. Rose's results have been questioned, but, whatever the magnitude, this literature redirected debate into a more balanced comparison of the microeconomic benefits and macroeconomic costs of currency union.

The benefits and costs may be changing over time. An increasing share of trade is being conducted along global value chains (GVCs) in which fragmented production is coordinated by a lead firm. This phenomenon is related to increased interest by trade economists and policymakers in the costs of doing international trade; as trade costs fall, increasing specialization by tasks and location of production stages in different countries becomes feasible. There is much more to trade costs than having to exchange currencies, but as the hard and soft infrastructure of international trade is improved, the relative burden of crossing currency boundaries is increasing.

2.1 Optimum Currency Areas

Optimal currency area theory dates from Mundell (1961). The optimum area is where, at the margin, the microeconomic benefits from a larger currency area are equal to the marginal costs of reduced macroeconomic policy effectiveness. The microeconomic benefits from a larger currency area in terms of reduced transactions costs, elimination of currency risk on international trade and foreign investment, greater transparency and ability to compare prices over a larger area are obvious but difficult to measure. The macroeconomic costs of a larger currency area concern lack of flexibility as monetary policy must be one size fits all, which is problematic if members of the currency union face asymmetric shocks.

In practice, the OCA literature has been dominated by macroeconomists arguing about determinants of the effectiveness of macroeconomic policy.[3] Both the costs and benefits of currency union are difficult to measure but 'almost all the interesting stuff comes from looking at factors that might mitigate the costs arising from the loss of monetary flexibility that comes with adopting someone else's currency' (Krugman, 2013, 441). If factors of production are mobile, then asymmetric shocks within the currency area can be met by labour or capital relocating from the depressed area to the booming area (Mundell, 1961). If fiscal transfers are possible within the currency area, then asymmetric shocks can be mitigated by transfers (Kenen, 1969). Both of these arguments may explain why the USA is closer to an optimum currency area than the European Union. For McKinnon (1963), openness is a key determinant of the extent to which an independent monetary policy is possible; small open economies have the least effective exchange rate policies, because the changes in relative prices following a devaluation will quickly pass through the domestic economy.[4] Each of these arguments is plausible but taken together they are hard to operationalize to explain existing or future currency areas beyond the obvious unions involving microstates.[5]

---

[3] Krugman (1993) was a prominent dissident who emphasized the potentially large microeconomic benefits.

[4] Kenen (1969) lengthened the list of criteria which might be relevant. For Alesina and Barro (2002), the trade-off might be mediated by history and by geography, but otherwise their criteria are similar to those in the survey by Tower and Willett (1976) or in the textbook treatment of de Grauwe (2020).

[5] McKinnon's openness argument explains currency unions involving microstates like Andorra, Monaco or San Marino, and small countries like Lichtenstein (that uses the Swiss franc), Timor-Leste (that uses the US dollar) or Brunei Darussalam (that uses the Singapore dollar), which would have little macroeconomic policy independence with a national currency. An independent currency would also impose large microeconomic costs as international trade would involve significant foreign exchange transactions costs for microstates' currencies.

More challenging than evaluating the costs and benefits of currency union and the arguments over macroeconomic policy effectiveness has been the limited testing of whether OCA theory explains actual currency domains (Pomfret, 2005). Kreinin and Heller (1974) synthesized the various OCA criteria into the single question of whether a country could better deal with external imbalance through devaluation or through adjustment of domestic demand. Their conclusion was that Italy, Sweden and Switzerland were the three OECD countries most likely to abandon their national currencies. Forty-five years later, only one of the three has done so, while ten of the 'less likely' countries have abandoned their national currencies. There has been little else in the way of serious testing of OCA theory.

Since the 1950s, despite the increasing openness of national economies and increasing capital mobility, which are both unambiguous pressures for larger currency areas according to OCA theory, the number of currencies has increased substantially and the geographical size of currency domains has shrunk correspondingly. Clearly, the exogenous increase in the number of countries drove the number and size of currency areas, and the OCA criteria were of little relevance for explaining the pattern.

Frankel and Rose (1998) have argued for a two-way relationship between trade intensity and a common currency, so that there is endogeneity in currency area formation or bilateral trade. In the data used in this and other papers by Rose (e.g. the influential Rose (2000) paper), the countries in currency unions are not from a random draw. Several authors (Persson, 2001; Kenen, 2002; Nitsch, 2004) have shown that the currency union members are smaller and more open than their natural comparators, and that history (usually in the form of colonial background) matters. Glick and Rose (2002) identify temporal correlations between changing currency union status and bilateral trade flows, but usually currency union break-up is associated with other events which disrupt trade; Nitsch (2003) showed that, out of some sixty cases of post-1947 currency union dissolutions in the Glick-Rose dataset, over two-thirds broke up within a decade of the end of a colonial relationship.[6] Thus, even the idea that OCA criteria can become self-fulfilling *ex post* due to feedbacks is unconvincing.

The overwhelming global pattern is one country one currency; that is, currency areas are determined by national boundaries. A few small economies

---

[6] In tranquil currency union changes, notably Ireland's secession from its currency union with the UK in 1979 and subsequent participation in the process leading to the euro, the impact on bilateral trade is unclear. Thom and Walsh (2002) found that breaking the currency union did not have an adverse impact on Ireland–UK trade, while Fitzsimmons et al. (1999) found that trade between Ulster and Ireland after 1979 was greater than predicted by a standard gravity model, despite the absence of a common currency.

use another country's currency (e.g. Brunei, Timor-Leste, Lichtenstein) and virtually no country has multiple currencies that are all accepted as legal tender. Ministates use a foreign currency because the transactions costs of a national currency would be too high and because they have very limited macroeconomic policy independence even if they had their own national currency. Otherwise, countries want control over their monetary policy agenda.

The benefits of a common currency are not only that it reduces transactions and search costs in the private sector. The benefits also apply to the public sector. Nations do not tolerate multiple currencies because they would make public revenue and expenditure decisions difficult. Once the national budget has been negotiated, the political balance would be upset if each province had its own currency that could change in value.

The arguments about control over the monetary policy agenda and about the content of fiscal policy differ from the emphasis of OCA theory on a trade-off between the microeconomic transactions costs benefits of a wider currency area and the macroeconomic cost of losing control over macroeconomic policy instruments. The first set of policy arguments have become increasingly relevant to the European Union as the member states' views on monetary policy converged in the 1980s and as the EU moves towards closer union with a more complex union budget.

2.2 A Common Currency and Bilateral Trade

Andrew Rose (2000) used a gravity model to compare the trade between countries with a shared currency and trade between countries without a shared currency. The gravity model, which hypothesizes that trade between two economic units depends on their economic size and the distance between them, had been developed by Dutch economic planners in the 1950s. In its simplest form, the gravity model is:

$$T_{i,j} = f(Y_i, Y_j, D_{i,j})$$

where the subscripts i and j refer to a pair of countries, $T_{i,j}$ is the bilateral trade between i and j, Y_i and Y_j represent the economic size of the two countries, and $D_{i,j}$ is the distance between them. The planners liked the model because it forecast future trade flows well, but other economists showed little interest because the results seemed obvious.

Modern use of the gravity model dates from the 1990s and especially the article by McCallum (1995) who analyzed bilateral trade flows among US states and Canadian provinces. McCallum found that the simple gravity model explained trade between two US states or between two Canadian provinces well, but trade between a state and a province was far smaller than predicted. Including a dummy variable for trade that involved crossing the border improved the statistical results and illustrated the economic importance of the US–Canada border even though it was one of the world's most open.

McCallum's paper was followed by many other papers using the gravity model to find deviations from the simple specification – when the force of gravity is 'unconstant' (Baldwin and Taglioni, 2006). Rose (2000) was one of the first of these papers. He included a dummy variable that took the value of 1 if two countries shared a common currency and 0 if they did not. The dummy's coefficient was statistically significant and implied that sharing a common currency, on average, tripled bilateral trade between a country-pair.

Rose's paper can be criticized for its econometrics and for its sample selection. Since 2000, gravity modelling has become more sophisticated (Anderson, 2011; Head and Mayer, 2015). Country fixed effects account for individual country factors affecting bilateral trade (e.g. North Korea trades less with other countries than might be suggested by global patterns of the impact of size and distance on bilateral trade flows [Anderson and van Wincoop, 2003]), and a range of estimating methods address the problem of zero observations (e.g. the Pitcairn Islands do not trade with Montserrat and, if the trade data are at a disaggregated level, individual commodities will not be traded between many country pairs). Rose (2000, 11 n. and 41) lists eighty-two countries and territories which used another country's currency or were in a currency union between 1970 and 1990; they are all small, with the most populous being the African CFA countries and Panama and Liberia, and many are quasi-countries (e.g. Isle of Man or Svalbard). On the whole, however, the finding that a common currency has a positive influence on bilateral trade flows appears to be robust, albeit with disagreement over the magnitude of the effect.[7]

In a post-euro assessment, Glick and Rose (2016) estimated that European monetary union boosted participants' bilateral trade by around 50 per cent. Glick (2017) separated the monetary union effect from the trade effect of EU membership and found that the independent effect of monetary union on trade of older EU members was about 40 per cent, and lower for more recent members. In sum, the euro appears to have had a large impact on bilateral trade, although it is difficult to translate this impact into the effect on GDP or on economic welfare more generally.

---

[7] Nitsch (2002) and Rose (2002) discuss the extent of overestimation in Rose's original results. Frankel (2010) found a 15 per cent increase in trade over seven years of euro use (1999 to 2006), which is far less than Rose's tripling but still substantial.

2.3 The GVC Phenomenon

When the Treaty of Rome was signed in 1957, most international trade consisted of goods that were often manually loaded and unloaded. By the time the euro came into existence, trade logistics had been transformed by the standardized container, door-to-door real-time tracking and other technical change. International production had also been transformed as many goods were manufactured along global value chains (GVCs) in which tasks were carried out in different countries and coordinated by a lead firm. GVCs depended on low transport and border-crossing costs and on reliable just-in-time delivery of components, to avoid the need for costly inventory holdings.

The emergence of the GVCs as a significant feature of world trade is dated by Baldwin (2016) to the 1980s.[8] One feature has been that most of the chains are regional rather than global, and are concentrated in three regions: East Asia, North America and Europe. A catalyst for the European GVCs has been enlargement of the EU to include countries with lower wage rates, that is, the Mediterranean enlargements of the 1980s (Greece, Portugal and Spain)[9] and, especially, the Eastern European enlargements of 2004 and 2007.

Among the Eastern European countries, the Czech Republic, Hungary, Poland and Slovakia participate the most in GVCs (Pomfret and Sourdin, 2018). This reflects many causal factors such as industrial traditions, the relatively high skill levels of the low-wage workers, good infrastructure and connectivity to lead firms in Germany, France, etc. Slovakia stands out and it is the only one of the four countries to be using the euro; Slovakia has the highest per capita car output of any country in the world, and the common currency must facilitate accounting of the components entering the country from elsewhere in the eurozone and of the value of the cars being assembled in Slovakia.

The GVC phenomenon is part of the expansion of international trade into increasingly specialized areas of comparative advantage where margins on each task are competitively squeezed and low costs of international trade are essential for profitability. As in the previous section, a common currency is one element of reduced trade costs. This helps to put some detail into the microeconomic benefits side of the OCA calculus and also, with the reduction of other

---

[8] On the emergence and characteristics of GVCs, see also Johnson and Noguera (2012; 2017) and UNIDO (2018).

[9] An early high-profile example was the Ford Motors decision in the 1970s, in anticipation of Spanish accession, to build a greenfield factory in Spain to assemble the Ford Fiesta from components sourced from across the European customs union. In the 1970s and 1980s, Malta, with preferential access to European Economic Community markets, became an assembly point for Wrangler jeans, with a quarter of the island's workforce employed in sewing jeans from imported inputs and exporting the jeans to the marketing center in Belgium which was the next stop in the value chain (Grech, 1978).

elements of trade costs and the rise of GVCs, provides a reason why a larger currency domain may be more popular in the twenty-first century than earlier.

3 The Werner Report and the Snake

The Treaty of Rome in 1957 paid little attention to monetary integration. The monetary chaos that followed the peace in 1945 was being resolved and the Bretton Woods system of trade with fixed exchange rates was about to come into full operation as exchange controls were loosened in western Europe. However, the system came under increasing stress during the 1960s as countries adjusted their exchange rates, notably the devaluation of the UK pound in 1967 and the devaluation of the French franc by 12.5 per cent and revaluation of the German mark by 9.3 per cent in 1969. The latter, involving the two largest members of the European Economic Community (EEC), triggered serious thought about economic *and monetary* integration.

3.1 The Werner Report

In post-1945 Europe, foreign exchange controls placed strict limits on access to and use of currencies, which was a serious impediment to trade. The European Payments Union was established in 1950 to facilitate trade by acting as a clearing house to settle trade imbalances among European countries, while currency restrictions were maintained for trade in US dollars. The system gradually became more flexible and the Payments Union terminated in 1958 when the currencies became convertible at fixed exchange rates. The Bretton Woods system based on fixed exchange rates was expected to last indefinitely. However, in 1969, a large devaluation of the French franc and revaluation of the German mark undermined expectations of exchange rate stability and raised questions of how well the customs union could function if exchange rates were not fixed.

At the December 1969, Hague Summit, the EC Council created an ad hoc committee of experts under the chairmanship of Pierre Werner to explore possibilities of stage-by-stage progress towards economic and monetary union. The work of the committee was presented in October 1970 in the Werner Report. The Report starts by setting out the final objective of economic and monetary union, which implies:

> Inside its boundaries the total and irreversible convertibility of currencies, the elimination of margins of fluctuation in exchange rates, the irrevocable fixing of parity rates and the complete liberation of national monetary symbols or the establishment of a sole Community currency. From the technical point of view the choice between these two solutions may seem immaterial, but

considerations of a psychological and political nature militate in favour of the adoption of a sole currency which would confirm the irreversibility of the venture. (Werner Report, 1970, 10)

The Report recommended a three-stage process to achieve monetary union by the end of the decade. During the first stage, commencing on 1 January 1971 and lasting for three years, fiscal and monetary policies would be coordinated and exchange rate fluctuations would be limited to a narrower range than those permitted in the Bretton Woods system. The second stage would involve financial market integration, removal of restrictions on capital flows between members, and short-term economic and fiscal policy coordination. The final stage would see the irrevocable setting of exchange rates, economic policy convergence and a community-level system of central banks. The expectation was that the three stages would be completed by 1980.

The Report's recommendations were adopted and the first stage began in April 1972. The delay was due to the 'Nixon Shock' in August 1971 when the convertibility of the US dollar into gold was suspended until a new set of exchange rates was agreed at the Smithsonian on 18 December 1971. The Smithsonian Arrangement, lauded by President Richard Nixon as 'the most significant monetary agreement in the history of the world', only lasted until February/March 1973, when the Bretton Woods system based on fixed exchange rates to the dollar broke down. The original participants in the first stage were the six original EEC members: Belgium, France, Germany, Italy, Luxembourg and the Netherlands. Denmark, Ireland, Norway and the United Kingdom joined shortly afterwards.[10]

3.2 The Snake in the Tunnel

Implementation of the Werner Report's recommendations took place against the background of the 1971–3 collapse of the Bretton Woods fixed exchange rate system. Under the December 1971 Smithsonian Agreement, exchange rates were fixed against the US dollar with a plus-or-minus 2.25 per cent margin of fluctuation. The European countries agreed that their bilateral exchange rates could only fluctuate by +/–2.25 per cent against each other. This meant that although the strongest and weakest European currency could in principle have a margin of 4.5 per cent if one were at the top of the US dollar range and the other at the bottom of the US dollar range, their European commitment would constrain them to a narrower band. The movement of the European currencies was conceived as a Snake within a tunnel; the wider tunnel represented the potential range of EEC

---

[10] Denmark, Ireland and the UK joined the EEC on 1 January 1973. Following rejection of membership in a referendum, Norway decided to remain outside the EEC.

national currencies' exchange rates against the dollar, while the narrower Snake captured the actual range of EEC countries' dollar exchange rates given the constraints on their bilateral exchange rate fluctuations.

The Snake broke down almost immediately in 1972–3. Denmark, Ireland and the UK withdrew in June 1972, a mere six weeks after they joined. Italy withdrew in February 1973 and France in January 1974. France re-entered in July 1975 but abandoned the mechanism in March 1976. Although most of the smaller countries maintained a fixed exchange rate against the German mark, the Snake was formally abandoned in 1976.

Circumstances were adverse. After twenty-five years of prosperity with generally stable exchange rates and prices, the early 1970s saw large, probably asymmetric, shocks. As well as the end of the Bretton Woods system of fixed exchange rates in 1971–3, prices of many commodities spiked (e.g. beef in 1972, oil in October 1973). Faced by unforeseen 'stagflation' (i.e. simultaneous increases in unemployment and in inflation), governments had different priorities and would not relinquish control over macroeconomic policy. For Germany, low inflation was paramount, while Italy and the UK prioritized low unemployment. France wanted to maintain the Snake and reduce unemployment. Fixed bilateral exchange rates between these four large countries were untenable.

The Snake participants faced the Impossible Trinity: a country cannot be open to capital flows and have an independent monetary policy and a fixed exchange rate. The four large countries were unwilling to compromise on monetary independence and so, even with the imperfect capital mobility of the 1970s, they could not maintain fixed exchange rates.[11] The smaller countries, recognizing that their freedom to pursue independent monetary policies was limited, were more willing to prioritize exchange rate stability.[12] As the Snake collapsed, the German mark rose in value against the US dollar, while the UK pound and the Italian lire fell in value as inflation rates increased (Figure 3.1).

A fundamental lesson from the Snake episode concerned the Impossible Trinity. If the European Communities were moving towards increased capital mobility and they wanted to maintain fixed exchange rates, then member countries would have to cede monetary policy independence. That lesson was not learned in the 1970s (or perhaps governments did not wish to learn it because they wanted to preserve monetary policy independence more than

---

[11] In the following decades, the desire to pursue diverging monetary policies led to the break-up of the ruble zone and currency disunion in former Czechoslovakia and former Yugoslavia (Pomfret, 2016).

[12] Denmark rejoined the Snake in October 1972, while Ireland maintained a fixed exchange rate with the UK (essentially a currency union that would not be broken until 1979). Both cases reflected the advantage of a fixed exchange rate with major trade partners – a position consistent with optimum currency area theory.

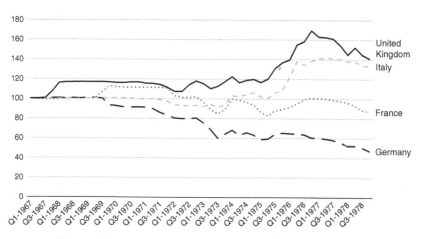

Figure 3.1 Exchange rates against the US dollar, 1967–78
Notes: exchange rates defined as amount of national currency to buy one US dollar, indexed to January 1967 = 100; increases indicate a weakening currency.
Source: author, based on data at https://stats.oecd.org/

they wanted to preserve the Snake). The lesson would be better understood in 1992 and a different policy conclusion would be drawn by most EU members.

4 The European Monetary System

Surprisingly soon after the termination of the Snake in 1976, German Chancellor Helmut Schmidt, French President Valéry Giscard d'Estaing and Chair of the EU Commission Roy Jenkins set about introducing a new version of the Snake in 1977–8. The European Monetary System (EMS) was effectively the same as the Snake with a few cosmetic changes: the Exchange Rate Mechanism (ERM) set each participating country's exchange rate in terms of a unit of account (the ECU) and a divergence indicator highlighted when an exchange rate was nearing the limit of its range.[13] The intentions resembled the Werner Plan in starting with fixed but adjustable exchange rates in 1979 and, after gradual tightening of the degree of fixedness and convergence of macroeconomic policies, replacing national currencies by a common currency. The difference was that the EMS fulfilled these intentions when it was replaced by the euro two decades later.

4.1 The EMS and Common Policies

Why did Schmidt, Giscard and Jenkins revive monetary integration so soon after the death of the Snake? And why did the EMS survive?

---

[13] The fluctuation margins around the bilateral rates were +/–2.25 per cent for all currencies, except the Italian lira, for which the margins were temporarily set at 6 per cent. The divergence indicator led some commentators to refer to the system as the Rattlesnake.

External conditions were no less unfavourable than in the 1970s. The start of the EMS coincided with the 1979–80 oil shock that was arguably as severe as the 1973 oil shock. The 1980s were characterized by trade disputes with Japan and newly industrializing Asian economies and by wild swings in the value of the US dollar, whose value increased rapidly against the German mark from 1.72 marks in January 1980 to 3.30 marks in March 1985, and then fell as dramatically in the second half of the 1980s to 1.50 marks in December 1990.

The European Economic Community's main common policy was the Common Agricultural Policy (CAP), which had been introduced gradually in the 1960s. For most farm products, the CAP protected farmers' revenues by maintaining price supports and ensuring, through a system of variable levies on imports, that domestic farmers could sell all that they produced at the fixed prices without competition from imported products. Over time, the generous support prices encouraged farmers to increase output and the price support commitment saw the EEC accumulating butter mountains, wine lakes and other surpluses as output exceeded demand. The surpluses incurred storage costs and were often disposed of to poor countries at discounted prices, effectively an export subsidy that incurred the ire of competing agricultural exporters such as the USA, Canada or Australia.

By the mid 1970s, the CAP accounted for two-thirds of the EEC budget, and the cost was rising as excess supply increased. Operation of the CAP within the European common market was disrupted by the more volatile exchange rates after the Snake collapse. To smooth out the domestic price changes that would follow exchange rate changes and trigger disruptive changes in internal trade, the EEC introduced artificial 'green exchange rates' that applied to agricultural product prices and adjusted more slowly than market exchange rates. Monetary compensation amounts (MCAs) were paid to or collected from countries suffering or benefitting from the gap between green and market exchange rates. The system was designed to stabilize prices, but it operated asymmetrically with a bias towards countries adjusting their green exchange rates quickly if the gap involved making payments and closing the gap at a more leisurely pace if they were receiving MCAs. In short, the CAP was becoming more complex and expensive in the presence of exchange rate changes.[14]

The argument could be generalized. Any budget that involves bargaining between representatives of different regions will be more open to dispute if the regions have independent currencies with volatile exchange rates. The balance of revenues and expenditures in each region's home currency will be changed

---

[14] Pomfret (1991) and Basevi and Grassi (1993) analyze the interaction between the CAP and the revival of monetary integration by Jenkins, Giscard and Schmidt. MCAs were phased out after the establishment of the EMS.

whenever exchange rates change. Hence, the pressure for a single national currency, as in the USA after independence or in Canada after Confederation.

4.2 The EMS in the 1980s

The EMS started life in March 1979 with eight participating countries: Belgium, Denmark, France, Germany, Ireland, Italy, Luxembourg and the Netherlands. The UK stayed outside the EMS so that it could retain monetary policy independence.[15] After fairly frequent realignments in the early years, realignments became less common (Table 4.1). Between January 1987 and the September 1992 crisis, there was only one realignment.

An important background contributor to the EMS's success was the convergence of ideas on macroeconomic policy (Pomfret, 2011, 148). The global reassessment of monetary policy and need to prioritize low inflation had already begun in the late 1970s by the Labour government in the UK and the Carter administration in the USA, although the monetarist approach to macro policy is most associated with Margaret Thatcher (elected UK prime minister in 1979) and Ronald Reagan (elected US president in 1980). In the early 1980s, the shift to a greater focus on price stability was almost universal whether by right-of-centre or by left-of-centre leaders such as François Mitterrand or Felipe Gonzàlez (elected prime minister of Spain in 1982).

The early years of the EMS saw few realignments (Table 4.1) but they were critical. In 1981, when François Mitterrand became the first Socialist President of France's Fifth Republic, he announced an expansionary economic policy program. With other EMS countries paying more attention to curbing inflation, Mitterrand's policies inevitably led to devaluation of the French franc. After three devaluations in eighteen months and tightening of foreign exchange controls, it became clear that Mitterrand had to either scale back on his expansionary macroeconomic policies or withdraw France from the EMS.[16] He chose the EMS in 1983.[17]

With a common perspective on prioritizing low inflation, the benefits of an independent monetary policy rather than a shared European monetary policy

---

[15] This decision meant that the Irish pound, which had previously been linked one-to-one with the British pound, became an independent currency, the punt.

[16] Howarth (2001, 55–81) describes this episode. The repeated devaluations offered speculators a one-way bet on the future exchange rate. After speculative attacks against the franc, exchange rate controls were at their tightest in March 1983; measures intended to prevent evasion via the use of leads and lags in current account transactions and to prohibit all forward exchange transactions by importers and exporters were introduced, and foreign travel allowances were drastically curtailed.

[17] France's position was key. After abandoning expansionary macroeconomic policies in favour of *le franc fort*, French policymakers became concerned that their monetary policy was being determined by the German central bank, the Bundesbank, whose focus on inflation made the German mark the benchmark EMS currency; in Table 4.1(b) changes in the mark's value are always positive and no other currency ever appreciated against the mark. The solution for France was to create the European Central Bank (ECB) which would supersede the Bundesbank on monetary policy (see Section 5).

Table 4.1 Exchange rate realignments within the EMS

(a) Number of realignments, 1979–95

Date	24/9/79	30/11/79	22/3/81	5/10/81	22/2/82	14/6/82	21/3/83	22/7/85	7/4/86
Number	2	1	1	2	2	4	7*	7*	5

Date	4/8/86	12/1/87	8/1/90	14/9/92	23/11/92	1/2/93	14/5/93	6/3/95
Number	1	3	1	3#	2	1	2	2

Note: * complete realignment; # on 14/9/92 the British pound and Italian lire left the ERM.

(b) Original members' realignments 1979–87, per cent change against the ECU.

	Bfr	dkr	DM	FF	Ir£	Lit	hfl
24/9/79		− 2.86	+2				
30/11/79		− 4.76					
22/3/81						− 6	
5/10/81		− 3	+5.5	− 3		− 3	+5.5
22/2/82	− 8.5	− 3					
14/6/82			+4.25	− 5.75		− 2.75	+4.25
21/3/83	+ 1.5	+ 2.5	+5.5	− 2.5	− 3.5	− 2.5	+ 3.5
22/7/85	+ 2	+ 2	+2	+ 2	+ 2	− 6	+ 2
7/4/86	+ 1	+ 1	+3	− 3			+ 3
4/8/86					− 8		
12/1/87	+ 2		+3				+ 2

Notes: Bfr = Belgium (& Luxembourg) franc; dkr = Danish krone; DM = German mark; FF = French franc; Ir£ = Irish punt; Lit = Italian lira; hfl = Dutch guilder.

diminished. Nevertheless, the success, after January 1987, of the EMS in creating the hard pegs envisaged in Werner's second phase is striking.[18] The 1980s were a decade when much else was happening in Europe starting with the multi-year dispute over the UK's budget contribution and the third enlargement to include poorer southern European countries Greece in 1981, Portugal and Spain in 1986.[19] The monetary integration could easily have been derailed.

The second half of the decade saw the Single European Act and rapid deepening of European economic integration. As part of that deepening, Commission President Jacques Delors argued in favour of taking the EMS to the next stage.

In June 1988, the EU Council set up a Committee for the Study of Economic and Monetary Union, chaired by Delors. The Committee's report, submitted in April 1989, defined the objectives of monetary union and indicated that they could be achieved in three stages. The objectives were complete liberalization of capital movements, full integration of financial markets, irreversible convertibility of currencies, irrevocable fixing of exchange rates, and the possible replacement of national currencies by a single currency (subsequently named the euro). In the first stage, from 1990 until 1994 the internal market would be completed and restrictions on further financial integration would be removed. In the second stage, from 1994 to 1999, the European Monetary Institute would be established to strengthen central bank co-operation and prepare for the European System of Central Banks (ESCB), the transition to the euro would be planned, the future governance of the euro area would be defined and economic convergence between member states would be achieved. In the third and final stage, from 1999 onwards, exchange rates would be irrevocably fixed and the transition to the euro take place. The ECB and ESCB would be established and binding budgetary rules would be implemented in member states.

The roadmap to monetary union was clear and was included in the Maastricht Treaty. The December 1991 Maastricht conference set targets for policy convergence, which were formalized in a treaty signed in February 1992 and ratified in 1993. The important point about giving the Maastricht agreement treaty force was that it indicated the political will in the majority of EU members to move to EMU when the feasibility of the Maastricht approach was being questioned by many commentators.[20]

---

[18] Artis and Taylor (1994) and Hu et al. (2004) provide evidence of the EMS's dampening effect on exchange rate volatility.

[19] After Greece, Spain and Portugal joined the EU, they initially maintained an independent exchange rate policy before formally acceding to the ERM in June 1989 (Spain) or the early 1990s (Portugal and Greece).

[20] Gros and Thygesen (1990) set out the case for the institutional approach, based on establishing a European Central Bank, as a necessary and feasible method of attaining EMU. Many academic economists underestimated the importance of political will in making EMU happen. A widely

The Maastricht Treaty set the conditions under which monetary union would start and specified entry conditions for using the common currency, including five convergence criteria which were intended to determine whether a country was ready to adopt the common currency:

1. **Inflation:** a country's inflation rate should not exceed the average of the three lowest inflation rates among EU countries by more than 1.5 percentage points.
2. **Long-term nominal interest rate:** this was not to exceed the average interest rate in the three lowest inflation countries by more than two percentage points.
3. **ERM membership:** before adopting the euro, a country must have spent at least two years in the exchange rate mechanism of the EMS without being forced to devalue.
4. **Budget deficit:** before adopting the euro, a country's budget deficit must have been reduced to less than 3 per cent of GDP.
5. **Public debt:** before adopting the euro, a country's public debt must be equal to less than 60 per cent of GDP.

The first criterion was intended to certify which countries had adopted a 'culture of price stability' and the long-term interest rate reflected the markets' assessment of long-term inflation. ERM membership signalled commitment to ceding monetary policy to the ECB. The last two criteria, which would prove to be the most controversial and most ignored, were intended to ensure sustainable macroeconomic stability without the temptation to monetize budget deficits or default on debt.

The Treaty provided the roadmap. However, following the road would encounter fresh challenges in the 1990s, stemming from the phasing out of controls on capital movement and German reunification in 1990.

5 The Maastricht Treaty and Creation of the Euro

In December 1991 in Maastricht, the governments of the twelve EU member countries approved the Treaty on European Union, declaring that they were 'resolved to achieve the strengthening and the convergence of their economies and to establish an economic and monetary union including, in accordance with the provisions of this Treaty, a single and stable currency'. The Treaty provided

---

read article by de Grauwe (1994) contained a section entitled 'The Maastricht Road Does Not Lead to EMU' and, given that the strategy devised in the Maastricht Treaty had proven 'impracticable', he proposed an alternative road. Similar dismissal of the Maastricht approach was voiced by many other European economists (cited by de Grauwe) and prominent US macroeconomists (e.g. Feldstein, 1992).

for the introduction of a monetary policy, implemented by a single and independent central bank, with price stability as a primary objective. It provided legal grounds for the establishment of a single currency and set convergence criteria which each member state had to meet in order to participate in the third stage of Economic and Monetary Union.

The spring and summer of 1992 was a period of global uncertainty even apart from the European questions of whether the German economy could absorb the eastern Länder without stoking inflation or whether the Maastricht Treaty would be blocked by national referenda. US economic conditions were uncertain in the run up to the 1992 elections and the futures of GATT (via the ongoing Uruguay Round negotiations) and of the proposed North American Free Trade Agreement were hard to predict.[21] In Japan, there were (as it turned out well-founded) doubts about the authorities' ability to stave off recession while managing the asset price deflation problem. On Europe's eastern border, the dissolution of the Soviet Union in December 1991 was followed by disarray in the fifteen successor states associated with the end of central planning, collapse of intra-republic trade and acceleration of inflation.

The process of moving from the European Monetary System (EMS) to monetary union began in 1990 with the phasing out of controls on capital movement. Without capital controls, an EU member would face a sharper choice between maintaining a fixed exchange rate with other members' currencies or having an independent monetary policy. With the increased weight of a reunited Germany, other countries feared that they would have to follow a German monetary policy that was inappropriate to their own situation.

The fears were realized in 1992. To finance reunification, the German government could create money, which it was reluctant to do for fear of inflation, or it could borrow. Increased German borrowing pushed up interest rates, leading in 1992 to an exchange rate crisis within the European Monetary System as other countries resisted having to match German interest rate increases. The 1992 crisis highlighted the Impossible Trinity or Trilemma: it is impossible to have free movement of capital, a fixed exchange rate and an independent monetary policy.

5.1 The 1992 Currency Crisis

By 1992, eleven of the twelve EU members were in the EMS. Spain and Portugal joined the EU in 1986 and formally entered the ERM in 1989 and

---

[21] In fact, the change of presidency after the 1992 US elections was followed by rapid conclusion of the NAFTA and Uruguay Round negotiations, and establishment of the World Trade Organization in January 1995. These positive outcomes for the global trading system were far from certain in 1992.

early 1992 after brief periods of their currencies shadowing the German mark. Greece had joined the EU in 1981 but would not be in the ERM until 1998. The process was most complex in the UK where Prime Minister Thatcher and Chancellor of the Exchequer Lawson had been in fundamental conflict over exchange rate policy since the mid-1980s, with Thatcher favouring a market-determined exchange rate and Lawson maintaining a peg to the German mark (Bonefeld and Burnham, 1996). Lawson resigned in October 1989, but the dispute continued within the Cabinet and his successor, John Major, brought the UK into the EMS in October 1990. The following month Thatcher was removed from power, and Major became Prime Minister.

The biggest challenge to the EMS exchange rate mechanism arose in the aftermath of German economic and monetary union that occurred in 1990. German economic and monetary union showed that, technically, monetary union was not difficult as the former East German Ostmarks were replaced by the West German Deutsche Mark. Few other lessons were learned, largely because currency union was considered inevitable in a reunified Germany; if East Germans were not allowed to trade in their worthless eastern marks for West German marks, they would flood the West German labour market with job-seekers. It was difficult to separate the impact of monetary union from that of other measures such as the imposition of uniform wages. Together, the one-for-one currency settlement and the uniform wages reduced the incentive to migrate from east to west and led to increased unemployment in East Germany.

German interest rates rose as the government borrowed to finance reunification. Pressure to follow the German interest rate increases in order to keep within the ERM limits led to major crises in other EMS members in September 1992. Italy devalued the lira on 13 September and left the exchange rate mechanism four days later. The UK delayed for a few more days, during which it lost large amounts of money to speculators who saw a one-way bet, before leaving the exchange rate mechanism on September 16. Spain and Portugal introduced capital controls; their currencies were devalued, and then the controls were removed.[22] Sweden left the exchange rate system after raising interest rates to 500 per cent. The uncertainty continued in 1993; to restore stability and discourage speculation, the ERM margins were temporarily widened to +/− 15 per cent in August 1993, although Germany and the Netherlands agreed bilaterally to keep their currencies within the +/− 2.25 per cent margins.

The lesson drawn from the currency crisis was that fixed but adjustable exchange rates are unsustainable without capital controls. As part of the 1992

---

[22] The last five realignment episodes in Table 4.1(a) are dominated by Spain. The peseta was devalued by 7 per cent in September 1992, 6 per cent in November 1992, 8 per cent in May 1993 and 7 per cent in March 1995.

program, to create a single market, capital controls within the EU were being removed. Only two alternatives remained for EU members: the UK, Sweden and Denmark opted for independent exchange rates, and the other EU members gave up their monetary policy independence. Italy rejoined the ERM in November 1996 and Greece joined the ERM in 1998. Establishment of the European Monetary Institute on schedule in 1994 effectively terminated independent monetary policy for the participating countries.[23] A currency crisis in 1995, following depreciation of the US dollar which increased demand for German marks, was far less significant than that of 1992.

The political background to the majority's choice lay in an agreement between President Mitterrand of France, who required monetary union as the price of French acceptance of German reunification, and Chancellor Kohl of Germany.[24] The decision was resisted by the head of the German central bank, who feared that an EU central bank would be less committed to stable prices, but Chancellor Kohl prioritized the opportunity to reunify Germany peacefully within a stronger EU. For President Mitterrand, currency union meant that EU monetary policy would be set by a European central bank rather than by the German central bank. The agreement was included in the Maastricht Treaty with a timetable for currency union and criteria for membership in the common currency area.

5.2 Implementing Maastricht: The Convergence Criteria

None of the eleven countries that had committed to currency union met the convergence criteria in 1994. Nevertheless, their governments committed at the June 1995 Cannes summit to 1999 as the starting date for monetary union and at the December 1995 Madrid summit to calling the common currency the euro. After being proposed at the December 1996 Dublin summit, a Stability and Growth Pact (SGP) was adopted in 1997 with the aim of strengthening the monitoring and coordination of national fiscal and economic policies to enforce the budget deficit and public debt limits established by the Maastricht Treaty. The SGP has been modified since then, but the basic principle of surveillance and monitoring of the convergence criteria remains.

---

[23] The European Monetary Institute was charged with ensuring the coordination of member countries' monetary policies and providing surveillance.

[24] This was not a formal agreement (Bozo, 2005) but part of an ongoing accommodation between Kohl and Mitterrand from the December 1989 Strasbourg summit, where Chancellor Kohl committed to keeping Germany at the centre of the European integration process during the drive for German reunification, to the Maastricht Treaty two years later. Among other issues, Kohl wanted to give greater power to the European Parliament, which Mitterrand resisted, and Mitterrand wanted a common European foreign policy to address concerns about post–Cold War security, but this was fairly toothless in the Maastricht Treaty.

The fiscal restrictions criteria (3 per cent deficit/GDP ratio and 60 per cent debt/GDP ratio) apply to countries seeking admission and to current eurozone members. Fulfillment of the criteria was to be evaluated by late 1997, a year before the euro would replace the national currencies. In practice, the evaluation in 1997 was ignored. In 1998, the Council decided that eleven EU members qualified and, in July 2000, the Council agreed that Greece also fulfilled the convergence criteria. In sum, all the countries that wanted to adopt the euro qualified, even though over half of the first twelve adopters of the euro had debt ratios above 60 per cent.[25]

Under the SGP budgetary surveillance process, eurozone member countries submit economic data and policy statements for periodic review, and an early warning mechanism notifies countries of slippage; peer pressure is to be imposed on member states to honour their commitments. However, when commitments are not met, peer pressure has had little effect. In 2003, the largest eurozone economies, France and Germany, were in violation with no consequences and, in 2009, only Luxembourg and Finland fulfilled both criteria. Greece before 2010 manipulated its budget data to conceal the true fiscal situation, which invalidated surveillance. In sum, the SGP failed to address concerns about fiscal discipline in an effective way.

However, all countries that adopted the euro had reduced inflation and met the first of the five criteria (Figure 5.1). This is consistent with the monetary policy outlined in the Maastricht Treaty with its overriding emphasis on price stability: 'The primary objective of the ESCB shall be to maintain price stability. Without prejudice to that objective, it shall support the general economic policies in the

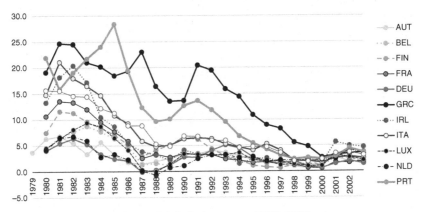

Figure 5.1 Inflation rates, 1979–2002
Source: OECD data at https://stats.oecd.org/

[25] The twelve countries included Finland and Austria, who had joined the EU in 1995, but not Denmark, Sweden or the UK.

Union in order to contribute to the achievement of the latter's objectives' (Article 282–2). The European System of Central Banks (ESCB) defines price stability as a year-on-year increase in the Harmonized Index of Consumer Prices for the eurozone below, but close to, 2 per cent, to be maintained over the medium term, which is commonly understood to refer to a two- to three-year horizon.

Since 1998, the ECB runs monetary policy for all eurozone members. At the end of 1998, the European Currency Unit exchange rates of the countries were frozen and the value of the euro, which superseded the ECU at par, was established. On 4 January 1999, the euro was introduced for financial transfers and the power to conduct monetary policy was transferred to the European System of Central Banks, under the aegis of the ECB. The initial eleven countries were Austria, Belgium, Finland, France, Germany, Ireland, Italy, Luxembourg, Netherlands, Portugal, and Spain. Greece adopted the euro in 2001. On 1 January 2002, the euro became legal tender in the participating countries and, by the end of February 2002, national banknotes and coins ceased to be legal tender.

The third condition in the Maastricht Treaty for joining the monetary union (i.e. at least two years of participation in the exchange rate mechanism), remains in place (Table 5.1). Since 1999, the mechanism is called 'ERM II' because it

Table 5.1 ERM membership

Pre-2000 EU members	Joined ERM	Left ERM	Post-2000 EU members	Joined ERM	Left ERM
Austria	1995	1999	Bulgaria	[1) c]	
Belgium/Lux[a]	1979	1999	Croatia	[2) c]	
Denmark	1979		Cyprus	2005	2008
Finland	1979	1999	Czech Rep		
France	1979	1999	Estonia	2004	2011
Germany	1979	1999	Hungary		
Greece	1998	2001	Latvia	2005	2014
Ireland	1979	1999	Lithuania	2004	2015
Italy	1979[b]	1999[b]	Malta	2005	2008
Netherlands	1979	1999	Poland		
Portugal	1992	1999	Romania		
Spain	1989	1999	Slovakia	2005	2009
Sweden			Slovenia	2004	2007
UK	1990	1992			

Notes: *a* Belgium and Luxembourg were already in a monetary union before 1979.
b Italy left the ERM in 1992 and rejoined in 1996.
c Bulgaria in 2018 and Croatia in 2019 have expressed the intention of joining the ERM II.

essentially replaced the exchange rate mechanism of the EMS. The exchange rate of a non-eurozone EU member's currency is set against the euro and a currency in ERM II is allowed to fluctuate only within a range of ±15 per cent with respect to its central rate against the euro. This is to ensure that exchange rate fluctuations would not impact on the economic stability of the single market.

Sweden negotiated an opt-out from the ERM when it joined the EU in 1995 but is formally committed to euro adoption. When Greece joined the euro in 2001, the Danish krone was left at that time as the only ERM member. Denmark remains in the ERM but has a formal opt-out from adopting the euro; the Danish central bank keeps the exchange rate of the krone within the narrower range of ± 2.25 per cent against the central rate of EUR 1 = DKK 7.46038, suggesting that maintenance of a national currency is cosmetic rather than economically useful to Denmark. The UK also had a formal opt-out from the euro but that became moot after leaving the EU in January 2020. All of the countries joining the EU since 2004 are bound to join ERM II and then adopt the euro, although the larger countries (Poland, Romania, the Czech Republic and Hungary) appear to be in no hurry.

6 The Euro Expanding

Two important reasons for the completion of currency union at the end of the 1990s, instead of collapsing as in the 1970s, were increased European economic integration after the Single Market had been established (and legitimized in the Maastricht Treaty) and general agreement that the prime target of monetary policy should be moderate inflation. Deeper integration magnifies the benefits in both the private and public sectors from a common currency. The European Central Bank has been successful in maintaining the inflation target.

The first decade of currency union was widely viewed as a success. The number of member countries increased from twelve in 2001 to sixteen in 2010 (and to nineteen in 2015). Even in the face of the financial crises that broke out in the USA, UK, Spain, Ireland and other small economies in 2007–8, and the decline in world trade from the end of 2008, the euro currency area was stable. Interest rate spreads across members were negligible until late 2009. Despite reported complaints in the media and nationalist opposition to the euro from populist parties, opinion surveys showed widespread satisfaction with the euro, although the level of support varied across countries.

Critics of the euro remained, especially in the UK which was not in the eurozone, and in the USA, although they tended to be subdued in the decade 1999–2009. The outbreak of the Greek crisis encouraged greater and more open scepticism and will be dealt with in the next section.

6.1 Increasing Membership of the Eurozone

Since 2002, seven EU member countries have joined the eurozone: Slovenia in 2007, Cyprus and Malta in 2008, Slovakia in 2009, Estonia in 2011, Latvia in 2014 and Lithuania in 2015. EU members not currently using the euro are required to join the exchange rate mechanism (ERM II) as a preliminary to meeting the convergence criteria and adopting the euro. However, of the eight EU members not using the euro, only Denmark participates in ERM II and Denmark has an opt-out clause from the euro. In 2003, Sweden voted in a referendum to stay out of the ERM, although it has no formal opt-out status and is expected to join by the ECB. Bulgaria sent a letter to the finance ministers of the eurozone member countries (the Eurogroup) in July 2018 expressing its desire to participate in ERM II. Croatia also sent a letter to the Eurogroup in early July 2019 on its desire to participate in ERM II and to adopt the euro by 2023. Kosovo and Montenegro have used the euro since 2002, although the EU Commission has expressed displeasure at non-members using the currency.[26]

Among the new EU members which joined between 2004 and 2013, there has been a split between the large countries, which have retained their national currencies and monetary independence, and the smaller countries, which were willing to join the ERM in 2004 or 2005 and after some years' delay (more than the two years' minimum) adopted the euro (Table 5.1).[27] The pattern is consistent with evidence that devaluation has little economic benefit for small open economies. The impact of euro adoption by these smaller EU members depended on the previous exchange rate regime; for example, euro adoption had a strong pro-trade effect on Slovakia which switched from a floating exchange rate to the euro but almost no impact on Estonia which had maintained a fixed exchange rate (Lalinsky and Meriküll, 2019).

6.2 The Eurogroup

The Eurogroup was established by the EU Council in 1997 as an informal meeting ground for policymakers associated with the euro. It reflected the need

---

[26] Four mini-states (Andorra, Monaco, San Marino, and Vatican City) have signed agreements with the EU to use the euro and issue their own coins, but they are not considered part of the eurozone by the ECB and do not have a seat in the ECB or the Eurogroup.

[27] Nguyen and Rondeau (2019) find that trade effects with the three largest eurozone economies (France, Germany and Italy) were more positive for the three early euro adopters (Slovenia, Slovakia and Estonia) than for the other new members from Eastern Europe, but Slovenia, Slovakia and Estonia were also more exposed to spillover shocks from eurozone economies.

for communication among a subgroup of EU members, given that some of the then fifteen EU members would not adopt the euro and the determination of those committed to the euro not to be held back by the non-participants.

A routine was established and continues today when the finance ministers of the nineteen eurozone countries meet the day before EU Economic and Financial Affairs Council (ECOFIN) meetings to discuss euro-related business such as the Stability and Growth Pact. In September 2004, the euro area finance ministers decided to elect a Eurogroup president to serve for a renewable term of two years (extended to two and a half years in 2009). Jean-Claude Juncker served as first president from 2005 to 2012. The Lisbon Treaty formalized the role of the Eurogroup in 2009.[28]

Since October 2008, the heads of state and government of the euro area meet twice a year in Euro Summits that set the direction and general terms for substantial and institutional reforms of the euro area. The October 2011 Euro Summit proclaimed continuity for the format of a regular, twice-yearly Euro Summit, as well as the central role for the Eurogroup, which will, together with the Commission and the ECB, remain at the core of the daily management of the euro area. The Eurogroup was established as the preparatory body for Euro Summits. This arrangement was formalized by Article 12(4) of the Treaty on Stability, Coordination and Governance in the Economic and Monetary Union (TSCG), concluded in March 2012. Second and more importantly, the 2011 Euro Summit statement established the position of a 'full-time Brussels-based President' of the Eurogroup Working Group (EWG), the main preparatory body of the Eurogroup, which is elected by and appointed by the Eurogroup. Thomas Wieser became the first person to be elected to this position for 2011–18, followed by Hans Vijlbrief. In order to reduce tensions between the upgraded EWG and the preparatory body of the Ecofin Council, and to increase efficiency and coordination, Wieser was also elected as President of the Economic and Financial Committee (EFC) in January 2012.[29]

The composition of the Eurogroup is identical to that of other eurozone bodies. The Board of Governors of the European Stability Mechanism that was established in October 2012 as the main source of sovereign loans from the

---

[28] While the Treaty itself does not mention the Eurogroup, Protocol No. 14 to the *Treaty on the Functioning of the European Union*, in conjunction with Article 137, recognized the legal status of the Eurogroup as the informal meeting format for euro area finance ministers. The protocol consists of only one paragraph that establishes the election, by the ministers, of a Eurogroup President for two and a half years. Protocol No. 14 also amended Council rules regarding the ECOFIN configuration of the Council such that on 'matters only affecting the euro area, only Eurogroup members are allowed to vote' (Braun and Hübner, 2019, 13).

[29] The EFC combines an advisory role vis-à-vis the Commission with its role as the preparatory body for ECOFIN.

EU typically meets during the afternoon of the Eurogroup's monthly meeting because composition is the same. The European Semester and all of the related macroeconomic supervisory measures discussed in Section 7.2 are also in effect managed by the Eurogroup.

During the early years of its existence, the Eurogroup was viewed as little more than a talking shop, although there were exceptional circumstances, for example, in November 2003 when France and Germany successfully forged a coalition among finance ministers to suspend the Stability and Growth Pact. The perception changed after 2009 when the the Eurogroup acted as the central – besides the ECB – decision maker and crisis manager in the sovereign debt crises, setting the conditions attached to European financial assistance to Cyprus, Greece, Ireland, Portugal and Spain. This active role continued to the 2018 drama in negotiations over Italy's national budget. The Eurogroup is not subject to normal EU procedures or responsibility to the Parliament, which has led to charges about lack of transparency and accountability (Braun and Hübner, 2019).

6.3 Popular Support and Ongoing Pessimism

The euro has the microeconomic benefits of a common currency: lower transaction costs, easier to make price comparisons, harder for monopolists to segment markets, and so forth. Although critics of the euro can be found, no government of a country in the eurozone has seriously considered exiting, including Greece at the height of its post-2010 financial crisis. Eurozone membership has increased from twelve countries in 2002 to nineteen EU members in 2020, and non-members Kosovo and Montenegro use euros. New EU members are required to adopt the euro, although they are allowed a transition period, which is turning out to be lengthy for some of the countries that joined in 2004 (i.e. the three largest economies: the Czech Republic, Hungary and Poland) and for all of the countries that joined in 2007 and 2013. Roth, Jonung and Nowak-Lehmann (2016) provide evidence of popular support for the euro in all EU countries using the euro, and lack of support for the euro in other EU members. Trichet (2019), one of the euro's architects, highlights its success.

Academic criticism has primarily come from US economists who argued in the 1990s that the common currency was a bad idea, that it would not be adopted, and if it were adopted disaster would follow (Jonung and Drea, 2009). Despite all of these predictions proving false, some continue to argue that the euro is a disaster, essentially on the grounds that countries need to pursue independent macroeconomic policies (e.g. Stiglitz, 2016) or because of the Greek crisis (see Section 7). Brunnermeier, James and Landau (2016) argue that the euro is doomed due to conflicting ideologies between France and Germany, although this seems similar to the ideological differences between blue and red US states and no US economist predicts demise of the dollar as the common currency of the USA.

Even a more moderate and better-informed US commentator, Barry Eichengreen, sees the future of European monetary union hanging in the balance. Eichengreen (2014) listed eight 'lessons' that had to be heeded. First, asymmetric shocks are inevitable in the EU and there need to be facilities to address these shocks given that they cannot be addressed by exchange rate changes. Second, monetary union requires a banking union, at least in establishing common deposit insurance schemes and resolution mechanisms for distressed banks that will break the 'doom loop'.[30] Third, the ECB must do more than follow a monetary policy rule, for example, by being a lender of last resort and ensurer of the stability in the banking and payments systems. Fourth, labour mobility as the answer to asymmetric shocks, as in Mundell's criteria for an OCA, is a mixed blessing if it takes the form of a brain drain from the poorer member countries. Fifth, fiscal transfers are politically implausible in today's EU because member governments are too aware of who would be net payers and their electorates will punish them and, sixth, need to be preceded by elimination of the debt overhang, which in turn requires (seventh) a mechanism for restructuring unsustainable debts. Eighth, 'monetary union is forever, more or less'; that is, breaking up the eurozone is probably more costly than maintaining and reforming the currency union. Thus, unlike the more strident doom-mongers, Eichengreeen does not see the euro as doomed to die, although he does believe that the design was flawed.

Eichengreen's first seven lessons highlight areas in which reform is needed in the eurozone. Such reforms are not clearly defined black-or-white issues, but rather the lessons indicate desirable directions of change. All countries regulate banking and other financial activities, but no set of financial regulations is perfect. For the EU, the need to strengthen financial institutional arrangements was highlighted by the debt crises that broke after late 2009. The ongoing debates about how to regulate will be reviewed in the next section after analyzing the evolution of the Greek sovereign debt crisis that dominated the decade of the 2010s.

---

[30] The risk of a banking crisis leads to an increase in the expected return on government bonds, which pushes the prices of bonds down with a negative impact on the balance sheet of holders of those bonds. This, in turn, increases the risks that a systemic crisis will happen. See Farhi and Tirole (2018).

7 The Sovereign Debt Crisis and its Aftermath

Between 2007 and 2010, the global economy experienced a series of major financial crises. The origins of the 2007–8 financial crises lay in financial reforms in the 1980s and 1990s. Deregulation and financial innovation combined with deposit insurance created moral hazard.[31] Increasingly risky real estate loans packaged in complex financial instruments would bring down major US investment banks and UK building societies. Similar patterns occurred in Spain and some smaller European economies (e.g. Ireland, Iceland and Latvia), where governments intervened to insure depositors in financial institutions and in some cases to nationalize insolvent banks; Ireland's debt problem was especially large because its government guaranteed not only depositors but all creditors of Irish banks. In the USA and UK, the financial crisis was over by 2009, although it had longer-lasting consequences for many people who lost out by becoming overindebted (and for a few who became rich). Although there was little financial contagion, financial crises in two of the world's five largest economies did trigger a global economic crisis through reduced global demand for goods.[32]

Within the EU, the 2007–8 financial crisis was notably absent in France, Germany or Italy, where financial deregulation had been more cautious. For the eurozone countries such as Spain and Ireland that experienced real-estate based financial crises, the crisis had little directly to do with the common currency. However, adoption of the euro played a part insofar as it facilitated borrowing to finance liquidity problems. Lenders assumed that, with no exchange rate risk, all eurozone government debt and blue-chip bonds were equally risky. This had led to interest rate convergence after the eurozone was established in 1999; all governments could borrow at German rates (Figure 7.1).

Greece was different because its debt crisis was essentially independent of the 2007–9 financial and economic crises and because it would become by far the most important eurozone sovereign debt crisis of the 2010s. In May 2010,

---

[31] Managers were tempted to make high-return risky loans because, if successful, the manager would receive a large bonus and if the loans were not repaid the manger would not have to cover the loss nor would depositors worry about losses if their deposits were insured by a government agency. The moral hazard danger had been evident in the US 1986–9 Savings and Loan crisis when taxpayers became the ultimate guarantors of S&L depositors' money (Pomfret, 2011, 143–5) but the potential application to US investment banks or UK building societies had been ignored.

[32] A striking feature (despite the 'Global Financial Crisis' label) was the lack of financial contagion, unlike the 1997–8 Asian Financial Crisis that led to Russian default and the collapse of Long-Term Capital Management in the USA. In 2007–9, events in the USA and UK triggered no financial crisis in South America, Asia, Africa, Australia and Oceania, Canada, or most of Europe.

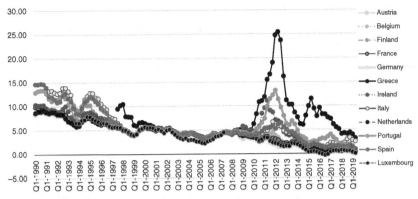

Figure 7.1 Interest Rates in eurozone Countries 1990–2019
Source: constructed from OECD data at https://stats.oecd.org/

Greece was the first eurozone country to request official financial assistance, raising awareness that all eurozone sovereign debt may not be equally safe. Emergency loans and packages were offered to Greece, and creditors identified Portugal, Italy, Ireland, Greece and Spain (the PIIGS) as potential problem cases. Interest rates diverged sharply in 2010–12 (Figure 7.1), contributing to the crisis by making the refinancing option more expensive for the indebted countries. Emergency loans and packages were offered to Ireland (November 2010, and February 2012), Portugal (May 2011), Spanish banks (July 2012) and Cyprus (May 2013). The major creditors were banks in EU countries without real estate bubbles (France, Germany and Netherlands), where 'prudent' banks which had avoided real estate lending and focused on 'safe' government loans or government-guaranteed loans.

The Greek crisis raised the question of the extent to which eurozone countries as a group should help a member country to avoid default. If there is joint responsibility, then this raises further questions about designing eurozone financial architecture that would reduce the possibility of financial distress in any member (or any systemically important financial institution in the euro-zone), give early warning of financial stress, and provide transparent rules for resolution of a liquidity crisis by the ECB or EU governments.

7.1 Greece

The fundamental cause of Greece's debt crisis was dismal fiscal management by Greek governments over several decades. The euro played a role because it allowed Greece to roll over pre-2001 debt by borrowing at low interest rates. The willingness of creditors to keep lending to Greece at these low rates allowed the country to increase the size of its external debt during the 2000s.

When Greece entered the eurozone in 2001, shortly before the issue of notes and coins on 1 January 2002, the government claimed to meet the criteria of a budget deficit equal to less than 3 per cent of GDP and a debt/GDP ratio of less than 60 per cent. The official budget deficit was supported by creative accounting (e.g. by moving pensions and other payments outside the budget). The reported debt ratio was accepted without question, even though for twenty years up to 2000 Greek government borrowing added up to more than double the sum of fiscal deficits, and this was continuing.

Greek governments continued to report manageable budget deficits and debt/GDP ratios between 2001 and 2009 despite some obvious reasons to question the reported figures. The public sector wage bill doubled between 2000 and 2010 in real terms. Many public sector areas, such as railways or schools, were hugely overstaffed. Prestige projects, including the 2004 Olympic Games, went far over budget with little legacy. The retirement age was reduced in many jobs to 55 for men and 50 for women. And many individuals and firms did not pay taxes.

In October 2009, a new government headed by George Papandreou entered office. Upon finding that the treasury was empty, the government decided to establish the true levels of revenues and expenditures. This was not easy. The government thought that the 2009 budget deficit was 3.7 per cent of GDP, but a fortnight later declared that it was 12.5 per cent, in other words, an annual shortfall of 31 billion euros. After further investigation, the deficit turned out to be 39 billion euros or over 15 per cent of GDP. According to *ex post* IMF estimates, the general government debt increased from 150 billion euros in 2001 to over 350 billion euros in 2011 (Figure 7.2). However, it was only in late 2009,

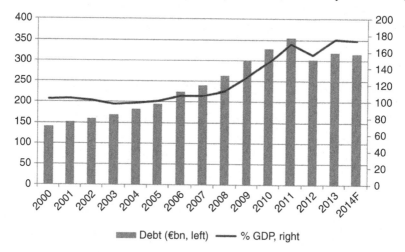

Figure 7.2 Greece, general government debt, in billion euros and as a percentage of GDP, 2000–4

Source: IMF Fiscal Monitor, April 2014

after the Papandreou government acknowledged that Greek data had been manipulated by previous governments, that the interest rate spread between Greek debt and that of other eurozone countries began to widen (Figure 7.1).

Warning bells sounded for holders of Greek government debt as the country faced default. Between April and June 2010, all the major credit-rating agencies downgraded Greek government bonds to 'junk' status. For EU countries whose banks were major creditors, the initial priority was to avoid Greek default and forestall failure of their banks.[33] In April 2010, over half of the bank holdings of Greek sovereign debt was held by French (33 per cent), German (15 per cent) and Dutch (5 per cent) banks (Roos, 2019, 236). In May 2010, the EU, the International Monetary Fund and the European Central Bank pledged 110 billion euros to help avert financial collapse in Greece, conditional on Greece cutting its budget deficit to 8.1 per cent of GDP by the end of 2010 and to 3 per cent of GDP by 2014. The 2010 bailout was important for providing a breathing space during which Greece could continue to service its debts while foreign banks could reduce their exposure to Greek debt.[34]

In May 2010, the Securities Market Programme allowed the European Central Bank to purchase distressed bonds. Between May 2010 and September 2012, the ECB purchased 210 billion euros of vulnerable eurozone members' bonds in the secondary market. Because the ECB could not fund budget deficits, it was not allowed to buy bonds directly from member governments, but the Securities Market Programme was a form of debt relief because it pushed down the price of a government's debt. In September 2012 the Securities Market Programme was replaced by the Outright Monetary Transactions scheme, which had a similar goal of providing bondholders with an exit strategy. Under both schemes, ECB activity was conditional on the primary issuer observing negotiated conditionality. This was a powerful weapon because, when the ECB did identify non-compliance and withheld purchases (e.g. with respect to Greek and Italian bonds in November 2011), the interest rate spread increased for the primary issuer pushing up the price of primary debt for both Greece and Italy, whose governments quickly backed down from the strategies that were ignoring previously negotiated conditions.

After the first bailout, it was clear that the solution would involve burden-sharing between creditors and the debtor. In the second EU-IMF bailout for Greece,

---

[33] Roos (2019, 228) reports that 'at the start of the crisis, some 80 per cent of Greek bonds were held by only a handful of systematically important banks in the rich eurozone countries, with the 10 biggest bondholders alone accounting for more than half of the country's outstanding obligations in mid-2011, and the 30 biggest accounting for over two-thirds.'

[34] According to Roos (2019, 244), between the first quarter of 2010 and the first quarter of 2011, German banks reduced their exposure to Greek debt by USD 9 billion and French banks by USD 13.9 billion.

approved by EU finance ministers in February 2012, the 130 billion euros in official assistance was accompanied by a 53.5 per cent debt write-down – or 'haircut' – for private sector holders of Greek bonds. However, by then the large foreign banks had much reduced their holdings of Greek debt and the burden was largely felt by domestic Greek creditors. As a condition of the second bailout, Greece was required to reduce its debt-to-GDP ratio from 160 per cent to 120.5 per cent by 2020.

For Greek residents, cuts to spending were labelled 'austerity', although it was inevitable that consumption of private and public goods and services would have to fall drastically from the debt-fuelled pre-2010 levels. Anger was exacerbated by inequality; rich people who had benefited from the boom and invested in offshore assets such as London apartments were sheltered from austerity measures, while people with only domestic assets had to downsize their car or house or worse. Despite popular resistance to the 2012 deal, the Greek government and its private creditors completed the debt restructuring on March 9, and a June 2012 election returned a government committed to the program. Nevertheless, there was no evidence that Greek governments were serious about reducing, let alone removing, the large public sector deficit. In 2010 Greece's general government deficit was 11 per cent of GDP, and the deficit/GDP ratio increased to 13 per cent in 2013. In sum, after the crisis struck, Greek governments were slow to tackle the public budget deficit, which was politically difficult and would be welfare-reducing. However, delay only extended the crisis.

The 2010–12 Greek crisis and EU response raise two questions: why not default on the debt and why not leave the eurozone? Neither Greece nor its creditors (nor other EU countries) wanted these outcomes. George Papaconstantinou, Greek Finance Minister at the start of the crisis, has stated that the government never considered default, a position which Roos (2019, 228) ascribes to Greece's need to finance the budget deficit or face even harsher immediate austerity, reliance on short-term trade finance to maintain crucial trade flows, and concern about Greece's reputation within the EU. The European Central Bank, which became more involved after May 2010, was also adamantly opposed to default. In September 2012, ECB President, Mario Draghi, re-committed to buying eurozone members' debt in the secondary market and doing 'whatever it takes' to forestall Greek default.[35]

Default would exclude Greece from almost all capital markets, including trade finance to cover the time-gap between exporters shipping goods and importers receiving and paying for goods. Compromise was less assured after

---

[35] Draghi's position was controversial because many saw the bond purchases as contravening clauses in the Maastricht Treaty that outlawed bailouts and ECB financing of members' debts. Bundesbank President Axel Weber and ECB Chief Economist Jürgen Stark resigned from the ECB's Governing Council over the bond purchases.

2012 because the rest of the eurozone countries – not just rich northern members who foot the bill, but also poorer countries that had implemented genuine public spending cuts[36] – were more willing to consider Greece defaulting and exiting the eurozone. Some partners may not have cared either way; the Greek economy is tiny in the EU context, about half of the gross metropolitan product of greater Paris (and roughly the size of that of greater Miami or Sydney).

The EU/IMF/ECB bailout aid in 2012 was to be distributed in tranches, to keep the pressure on Greece to honour its commitments. To secure release of the instalment of almost $9 billion in rescue loans due in July 2013, the government introduced austerity measures. Plans to put 25,000 civil servants, including teachers, municipal police officers and school janitors, into a 'mobility plan' by the end of the year, docking their wages ahead of forced transfers or dismissals, generated the most public anger, prompting labour unions to hold a general strike. The government survived and was able to re-enter the bond market in 2014, relieving some financial pressure. But austerity measures remained unpopular.

The government stood for renegotiation of bailout terms, debt cancellation and increased public spending. On 30 June 2014, Greece missed a €1.6 billion payment to the International Monetary Fund – the first developed country to default on an IMF payment. EU opinions were divided: ECB executive board member Benoît Coeuré insisted 'Greece has to pay, those are the rules of the European game', but French Finance Minister Michel Sapin warned that 'If this new government was elected, it's also because Greece has lost 25 per cent of its national wealth in the space of five years. That's extremely heavy, extremely hard for people to bear'. In January 2015, a coalition government was formed under the leadership of the left-wing Syriza Party. A July referendum in Greece voted for rejection of bailouts. Nevertheless, the government agreed to a third bailout, worth 86 billion euros, under terms that were more stringent than previous bailouts.[37]

In 2017, tensions over Greece's third bailout grew as the IMF warned that the country's debt was unsustainable and that the budget cuts that EU creditors were demanding would hamper Greece's ability to grow. EU representatives agreed to more lenient budget targets but declined to consider any debt relief. Greek

---

[36] Between 2010 and 2013, Latvia reduced its deficit/GDP ratio from 9 per cent to 1 per cent, Portugal cut its deficit/GDP ratio from 11 per cent to 5 per cent and Ireland cut its deficit/GDP ratio from 32 per cent to 6 per cent. Eurostat data on deficit/GDP ratios, as defined in the Maastricht Treaty: http://ec.europa.eu/eurostat/tgm/table.do?tab=table&init=1&language=en&pcode=tec00127&plugin=1

[37] Lim et al. (2019) provide an account of the evolving balance of power between Greece and Germany in the bailout negotiations of 2010, 2012 and 2015, emphasizing the crucial role of the IMF in providing impartial inputs on the capacity of Greece to service its debt and on the technical feasibility of conditions placed on Greece.

Prime Minister Tsipras agreed to implement deeper tax and pension reforms even as he faced domestic pressure over a weakening economy and rising poverty. A June 2018 plan allowed Greece to extend and defer repayments on part of its debt for another ten years and gave €15 billion in new credit. Greek Finance Minister Euclid Tsakalotos said it marked 'the end of the Greek crisis' and Prime Minister Alexis Tsipras claimed that 'Greece is once again becoming a normal country, regaining its political and financial independence'. Capital markets responded positively in July 2019, when Greece issued its first seven-year bond since 2010; the target of €2.5 billion was modest but offers exceeded €13 billion pushing down the yield to 1.9 per cent.[38] With Greece subject to enhanced surveillance for the next decade, reaction on the ground was muted. Greece will have to stick to austerity measures and reforms, including budget surpluses, for over forty years, and adherence will be monitored quarterly.

The overall picture is that Greece had been surviving primarily on loans from the eurozone since 2010, when it lost market access to funds because of a ballooning budget deficit, huge public debt and an underperforming economy, matched with an expansive welfare system. The country was plunged into an unprecedented recession from which it was only starting to recover in 2018, posting economic growth of 1.9 per cent after its economy had shrunk by more than 26 per cent since 2010. Wages had fallen by nearly 20 per cent since 2010; pensions and other welfare payments were cut by 70 per cent in the same period. The size of the public sector had been reduced by 26 per cent. Unemployment had dropped slightly but remained at 20 per cent, with youth unemployment at 43 per cent, sending thousands of young Greeks abroad. At almost 180 per cent of GDP, the €320 billion debt mountain still amounts to the highest debt ratio in the EU but Greece's borrowing costs stand at about 4 per cent, compared with 24 per cent at the peak of the crisis.

Although the Greek crisis cannot be separated from eurozone membership, it is unclear just how much the euro contributed to the crisis and its unfolding. The crisis would have hit sooner if Greece had not had the opportunity to borrow at German interest rates during the first decade of the twenty-first century. However, the euro did not cause the crisis in any meaningful sense; that has to be laid at the door of successive Greek governments and the banks who lent to Greece without recognizing the danger of loans turning bad. The unfolding of the crisis through the three bailouts between 2010 and 2015 has many similarities to the Latin American bailouts of the 1980s. Creditor banks, with the support of their governments, prioritized recovering as much of their loans as possible. The 2010 bailout provided a breathing space when debts

---

[38] 'Let the Good Times Roll', *The Economist* (London) 3 August 2019.

continued to be serviced while the foreign banks divested their Greek bonds. After 2012, the priority was to wind down Greek debt with as little fuss as possible, a process which involved transferring risk to domestic Greek banks and EU taxpayers. The ECB remained involved and used its monopoly over euro emissions and power to purchase Greek debt in the secondary market to pressure Greek governments to remain on track with the conditionality. Although the ECB was reported as threatening that Greece would have to leave the eurozone if it went off-track, that option – and indeed anything to do with the common currency – appeared not to be a driving force of the Greek debt crisis.

The Greek crisis did, however, impact the eurozone by invigorating discussion of banking and capital reforms that might be desirable in themselves and as pillars supporting the eurozone.

7.2 Reform in the Eurozone

The European Central Bank as it operated in the 2000s was responsible for monetary policy but lacked many other powers normally held by central banks. The ECB did not have power to act as lender of last resort to banks in difficulty. Financial regulation and supervision as well as monitoring the Stability and Growth Pact (SGP) were responsibilities of the EU Commission not the ECB. These areas needed reform as well as rethinking their administration; the SGP had been established at the same time as the single currency in order to ensure sound public finances, but it did not prevent the emergence of serious fiscal imbalances in some EU members. At the same time, many critiques of the eurozone's institutional structure questioned the prospects of currency union without a banking union or fiscal policy coordination. The Greek and other financial crises were a catalyst for rethinking the ECB's responsibilities and the institutional framework of the eurozone.

Fiscal rules, as in the convergence criteria for eurozone membership, are non-transparent, procyclical and divisive. Some progress on definitions and transparency had been made in the Maastricht Treaty and by Eurostat, but Greece evaded them in the 2000s. Fiscal rules can be procyclical because during recessions budget deficits automatically increase as tax revenues fall and social security payments increase; if the deficit passes the 3 per cent threshold, the government may be obligated by the fiscal rules to cut spending or raise taxes when they want to use expansionary fiscal policy to stimulate economic activity. Among other issues, this raises the question of whether automatic stabilizers (e.g. unemployment insurance) should be shifted to the EU level. The rules are divisive because national governments differ on priorities such as how they weight unemployment versus inflation. Helping countries with a liquidity crisis by giving loans conditional on fiscal adjustment often leads to a populist backlash and having rigid bailout rules exacerbates crises (as in Greece in 2010–12 and 2015).[39] To some extent, this is about subsidiarity; what are EU issues and what are national issues?

Legislative packages to strengthen the Stability and Growth Pact have been the central pillars of the EU's efforts during the 2010s to improve its macroeconomic governance. The SGP has been reformed through a series of measures to improve monitoring of eurozone members' macroeconomic policies, starting with the European Semester, introduced in 2010 and revised in 2015, which ensures that eurozone members discuss their economic and budgetary plans with their EU partners at specific times of the year. The 'Six Pack', which became law in December 2011, introduced a new macroeconomic surveillance tool, the Macroeconomic Imbalance Procedure, and the 'Two Pack', which entered into force in May 2013, requests eurozone members to present draft budgetary plans for the following year in mid-October.[40]

The Intergovernmental Treaty on Stability, Coordination and Governance in the Economic and Monetary Union (TSCG) that was formally concluded on 2 March 2012, and entered into force on 1 January 2013, reinforced the procedural reforms. The TSCG is a stronger version of the Stability and Growth Pact. The main provision is the requirement to have a balanced budget rule in domestic legislation, referred to as the Fiscal Compact. Out of the twenty-five contracting parties to the TSCG, twenty-two are formally bound by the Fiscal Compact (the nineteen eurozone countries plus ₊Bulgaria, Denmark and Romania).[41] For countries bound by the Fiscal Compact, the national budget has to be in balance under the treaty's definition, which is a more nuanced version of the SGP's 3 per cent of GDP criterion.[42] The

---

[39] Countries rarely have an insolvency crisis. Choices exist about the price of haircuts (Cruces and Trebesch, 2013) and about enforcing a hard or soft default (Trebesch and Zabel, 2017). Roos argues that the power of creditors to prevent a hard default has increased substantially in recent years.

[40] More detailed information on these procedures can be found on the EU Commission's website: https://ec.europa.eu/info/business-economy-euro/economic-and-fiscal-policy-coordination/eu-economic-governance-monitoring-prevention-correction/european-semester/framework/eus-economic-governance-explained_en

[41] Croatia, the Czech Republic and the UK did not sign the accord. In December 2011, British Prime Minister David Cameron went as far as exercising a veto on incorporating the TSCG into the Lisbon Treaty, to the disgust of most other EU leaders who saw his action as a sop to anti-EU members of Cameron's party in the UK. The contracting parties have continued to seek ways of incorporating the TSCG into EU law despite the strong opposition of the UK, which has become moot after Brexit, and the Czech Republic.

[42] The treaty defines a balanced budget as a general budget deficit not exceeding 3.0 per cent of GDP and a structural deficit not exceeding a country-specific medium-term budgetary object-ive which at most can be set to 0.5 per cent of GDP for states with a debt/GDP ratio over

countries must establish an automatic correction mechanism to correct poten-tial significant deviations from budget balance and a national independent monitoring institution to provide fiscal surveillance. The TSCG also contains the 'debt brake' criteria outlined in the Stability and Growth Pact, which defines the rate at which debt levels above the limit of 60 per cent of GDP shall decrease.

Although commentators have criticized the treaty for being 'long on good intentions but rather short on substance' (Gros, 2012), the cumulative impact of the procedural innovations and the Fiscal Compact represent a significant step towards increased fiscal co-operation. The regular cycle of meetings and report-ing that tracks members' budget drafts through the year gives the TSCG more enforcement substance than the original Stability and Growth Pact. However, the arrangement is still inter-governmental rather than a fiscal union and its ability to pre-empt future crisis will only be apparent when the next pre-crisis situation occurs.

In 2010, the EU created two temporary funding programmes, the European Financial Stability Facility and the European Financial Stabilisation Mechanism, that provided financial assistance conditional on the implementation of reforms to Ireland and Portugal between 2011 and 2014, and short-term bridge loans to Greece in July 2015. In September 2012, these temporary programmes were replaced by the European Stability Mechanism, an intergovernmental organiza-tion providing instant access to future financial assistance programmes for euro-zone members in financial difficulty, with a maximum lending capacity of €700 billion in the form of loans or as new capital to banks in difficulty.

In June 2012, the EU committed to establishing a banking union. In 2013, a Single Resolution Mechanism was introduced for winding down banks in difficulty. A June 2018 Summit on Euro Area Reform took two major steps towards banking and fiscal reform by referring to a European Deposit Insurance Scheme, to be introduced after sufficient reduction in banks' legacy risks, and by commitment to strengthening the European Stability Mechanism through pre-crisis assistance and more flexibility in debt restructuring. Missing items at the summit included agreements on limits to how much a bank can lend to a single sovereign borrower, on how to improve and enforce fiscal rules, and on how to pursue macroeconomic stabilization given that eurozone member gov-ernments no longer have independent monetary policies.[43] Other ongoing

---

60 per cent or at most 1.0 per cent of GDP for states with debt levels under 60 per cent of GDP. If a state suffers a significant recession, it will be exempted from the requirement to deliver a fiscal correction for as long as the recession lasts.

[43] Eichengreen (2019) focuses on whether pre-agreement between Germany and France on these issues is enough to forge consensus among the nineteen eurozone member countries.

financial issues include links between banks and sovereign borrowing; incomplete banking union leaves banks vulnerable to national government pressure.

Lender of last resort to banks remains a national responsibility. Farhi and Tirole (2018) have demonstrated that this creates a doom loop that transforms a bank crisis into a public debt crisis. Even if lending to distressed banks is under the European Stability Mechanism, the liability for repayment is national. If the ECB lends to banks facing a liquidity crisis through its Emerging Liquidity Assistance facility, it does so through the relevant national central bank and, in principle, only to banks that are deemed to be solvent. This is not an unconditional lender of last resort guarantee and because liability is national it perpetuates the doom loop.

In 2018, the European Commission proposed creation of Sovereign Bond-Backed Securities (SBBS), a new financial instrument that would take the form of liquid assets backed by a pre-defined pool of eurozone central government bonds. SBBS are a market-led solution to promote financial integration, to reduce the 'home bias' in investors' portfolios and to facilitate the diversification of sovereign exposures. SBBS should contribute to financial sector stability by further weakening the link between banks and their governments by allowing banks to invest in a type of low-risk liquid asset that is less dependent on the solvency of one particular nation state while still benefiting from a more favourable regulatory treatment than traditional securitization products.[44]

The measures described here are difficult to assess in a vacuum. Their effectiveness depends upon implementation as well as on declarations of intent and the strength of implementation may only be revealed when the next crisis occurs. Further areas under discussion include strengthening banking regulation via the European Securities and Market Authority (ESMA) to oversee concentration of lending in government securities, and a common approach to non-performing loans. Instead of focussing on the current fiscal deficit, rules could be set for long-run increase in government spending relative to long-run income growth. Credible collective action rules in sovereign debt crises to prevent holdout by individual creditors could be introduced.

In sum, a consequence of the sovereign debt crises that broke out after late 2009 has been serious rethinking of the appropriate institutions to accompany a single currency in a more deeply integrated EU. The process is messy because the EU is neither a federal nation like the USA or Canada nor a currency union of otherwise economically independent countries like the Central African CFA Franc Zone. Some of the measures described may work

---

[44] SBBS will enjoy the same regulatory treatment as national eurozone sovereign bonds in terms of capital requirements, the eligibility for liquidity coverage and collateral, and so forth.

and others may not, but the point is that together they represent a tentative step towards more integrated approaches towards fiscal policy, a banking union and sovereign debt relief.

7.3 Debt Default in a Currency Union

Despite frequent reports that debt default would force Greece to abandon the eurozone, there is no inevitable link between debt default and exiting a currency union. A country may choose to leave a currency union in order to regain control over monetary policy and be able to adjust exchange rates (as in the ruble zone) or there may be an amicable currency divorce by countries seeking diverse monetary policies (as when the Czech and Slovak koruna were separated on 8 February 1993), but it will not have to leave inevitably just because it defaults on debts. There is currently no mechanism for a country to leave voluntarily or be ejected from the eurozone.

In the 1840s, eight US states and the territory of Florida went bankrupt but remained in the dollar currency area. Current reading of the US Constitution is that it is illegal for states not to meet their debts because they have a constitutional duty to pay their bills in full. When a 'restructuring' by Arkansas in 1934 did not satisfy creditors, they were eventually rescued by a federal purchase of their assets at par, that is, a de facto bailout of a defaulting state. Since 1937, US cities and other municipalities can seek bankruptcy under Chapter IX of the Bankruptcy Act (there have been over 600 cases, of which Detroit in 2013 with debt of $18.5 billion was the largest), but states are explicitly excluded. After the Commonwealth of Puerto Rico, which uses the US dollar, ran into financial difficulty, Congress passed the Puerto Rico, Oversight, Management, and Economic Stability Act (PROMESA) in 2016, under which the US President could appoint a financial oversight board to restructure the territory's debts.

In Canada, there is no constitutional obstacle to provincial default or to bailouts. Canada's only default on a province's debt was by Alberta in 1936. In recent discussion of whether New Brunswick may be unable to service its debts, the common view is that the federal government would bail the province out in order to avoid damage to Canada's reputation for fiscal probity.

None of these historical events threatened the composition of the currency unions of the USA, Puerto Rico and the USA, or Canada. The EU is different from the Puerto Rico case insofar as it is unlikely that a member state would allow the EU to appoint an independent board to manage its public finances. The EU situation could be a little different than the US position that states must sort out their own debts (a strategy recommended by Mayer (2012)) or than the

Canadian situation where the federal government may choose to support a province in financial difficulties, either of which is consistent with the indebted state remaining in the common currency area.

7.4 Was the Greek Debt Crisis a 'Euro Tragedy'?

After Act One – adopting the euro in 2001 – Greece enjoyed a decade of prosperity (Act Two). This contained the seeds of the final act, in which Greek residents lived through a decade of much-reduced living standards.

The common currency encouraged Greece's creditors' unwarranted belief in the safety of their loans, but this reflected the foolishness of the creditors who would in 2012 pay for their error. The common currency allowed Greek governments to borrow cheaply but does not justify the awful fiscal management both in operational terms (poor public service management) and on prestige events such as the 2004 Olympic Games. The euro clearly had a role in the play, but it was not a lead actor.

Would Greece have weathered the crisis better if it had reintroduced the drachma and devalued? This seems unlikely given the openness of the Greek economy.[45] After devaluation, higher prices of imported goods and services would quickly pass through to the domestic economy adding to firms' costs and triggering wage increases, so that any competitiveness benefits for Greek exports would be quickly eroded. Meanwhile, existing debt and any new debt would be denominated in euros (or another international currency) and more drachmas would be required to service the debt after devaluation. As it was, austerity and falling wages and rental values made Greece a more competitive tourist destination but the net impact on revenues from tourism was limited.

What about other euro members? The main concern in 2020 is Italy, which has the largest external debt by value and has had a stagnant economy since 1992. Populist politicians blame the euro, although Italy's economic malaise predates the euro. It is implausible that lire devaluations would have impacted positively on this record of relative decline. The euro has, however, been an easy scapegoat that diverts attention from the need for reforms that might involve short-term concentrated negative effects.

The euro has, however, not been a neutral feature of the sovereign debt crises. By ending exchange rate risk, the common currency eases profligate countries' access to foreign credit. In a federation, there is also a presumption that no part will be allowed to renege on its obligation to supply basic public services. In the

---

[45] Several commentators emphasize the difficulty of carrying out a conversion of euros to drachmas in a crisis situation. Any hint of a return to the drachma, to be followed inevitably by devaluation, would trigger a massive run on banks to obtain euros and capital flight from the country.

USA, cities or states can and have gone bankrupt. In such cases the federal government takes over, typically providing a technocratic leadership to manage the city or state until it is once again able to operate independently. On occasion, EU countries have gone down this path (e.g. Italy's appointment of the Monti government in November 2011), but it has been done by domestic choice; the EU is not sufficiently integrated that an external administrator can be appointed by the Commission or Council to run a member country's economy. The EU tried to forestall the administrator option by setting limits to budget deficits and to borrowing, but these limits have been exceeded by many members, including by France and Germany, without serious punishment.

To return to positive aspects of the euro, a single currency is part of the ever-deeper economic integration and creation of a single EU market. The euro is also key for negotiating the EU budget, which is now set for six years after substantial bargaining. Not all EU members use the euro, but the majority do; in a two-tier EU with a more integrated euro-using core and a non-euro-using periphery, the former will dominate.[46] The two-tiers are already evident in the increasing importance of the Eurogroup since its establishment in 2009. The monthly Eurogroup meeting, on the eve of the Economic and Financial Affairs (ECOFIN) Council meeting, is increasingly viewed as the place where the nineteen eurozone countries predetermine outcomes for the ECOFIN meeting of all EU members. Eurogroup President Jeroen Dijsselbloem was an increasingly visible and important figure in Greek crisis and Brexit debates.

Deeper integration will reinforce the need for a common currency in which to denominate the EU budget and financial aspects of policies. The eurozone's design has been criticized for the lack of supporting institutions, but the historical norm has been for establishment of such institutions to follow rather than precede a currency union. That process may be slower and more convoluted than in a newly created federal nation, but the steps are being taken. The Greek crisis was a tragedy for the majority of Greek citizens but it was also the prologue to strengthening the eurozone's financial institutions and arrangements.

8 Conclusions

Crisis management in the 2010s and response to the need to address banking and financial sector reform have dominated thinking about the euro. However,

---

[46] By 2018 population, the eurozone countries contained 342 million of the EU's 513 million people. Subtracting the UK, the numbers are 342 million in eurozone countries and 105 million outside the eurozone. The balance will shift further if the smaller non-euro countries adopt the euro, as is likely for Croatia (4 million) and Bulgaria (7 million) and possible for Demark (7 million) and Sweden (10 million), leaving only Poland (38 million), the Czech Republic (11 million) and Hungary (10 million) outside.

those issues are essentially about making the monetary and economic union function better in future and do not address the deeper question of why the common currency was introduced.

The global pattern is that currency domains follow nation-building: an integrated nation recognizes a single currency. Currency union is a component of the ever-deeper economic integration of the European Union. The precise timing of euro adoption was affected by specific challenges in the 1990s and eurozone membership has reflected differing commitments to the ideal of a united Europe (notably the UK's opposition to the common currency and the reluctance of more nationalist governments in Hungary and Poland to adopt the euro), but the direction of change from the Werner Plan to the euro was consistent.

Currency union was not inevitable. If there are irreconcilable differences in desired monetary policy (as in Czechoslovakia in 1990 or Yugoslavia in 1992) or gross macro mismanagement (as in the ruble zone in 1992–3), then a common currency is unsustainable. In these three cases, the end of currency union was associated with the end of political union and creation of new independent states. Similarly, monetary policy differences accounted for the failure of the Werner Plan in the 1970s but were not associated with the run-up to and operation of the euro because there has been general agreement among eurozone members on the priority of maintaining price stability and ECB management of monetary policy has been competent. In its first two decades, despite financial crises, the euro faced no existential challenge. Eurozone membership increased from eleven to nineteen countries, with no exits.

One casualty of Europe's currency union is, or should be, optimum currency area theory. OCA theory is a useful heuristic to highlight the potential trade-off between the microeconomic benefits and the macroeconomic costs of currency union, but it is neither a good explanation of the size of currency domains nor a good guide to policymakers embarking on currency union. The policies required for the better functioning of the eurozone are scarcely mentioned in the OCA literature and it is unsurprising that they are being implemented piecemeal and largely in reaction to crises.

Nevertheless, OCA theory retains a strong appeal, especially among US economists. Krugman (2013, 439) argues that 'the euro has become an economic trap, and Europe a nest of squabbling nations. Even the continent's democratic achievements seem under stress, as dire economic conditions create a favourable environment for political extremism'. According to Krugman, the blame for this dystopian outcome could have been predicted by OCA theory; it results from adopting a common currency when labour was immobile and large fiscal transfers impossible. Ironically, from a 2020 perspective, the description of squabbling regions and political extremism seems more appropriate to the US dollar currency area than to the eurozone. The dire economic condition of Greece (and Italy) in the 2010s was primarily due to poor domestic economic management that predated the common currency and their situation would have remained dire if more people had emigrated (especially if adverse selection led to a brain drain) or if their EU partners had provided transfer payments.

The events and rethinks surrounding the Greek crisis (Section 7) are driving the policy reforms in a largely positive way, rather than being the prelude to collapse of the eurozone. After all, the successful currency unions of the USA and Canada were not aligned with OCA criteria in the late 1700s or the mid-1800s and creation of banking and fiscal unions was not without hiccups. This is the kernel of Eichengreen's aphorism that *Monetary Union is Forever: More or Less*; the euro currency union may have done better if it had a different starting point, but once in place it is unlikely to collapse unless member countries develop diverse ideas of appropriate monetary policy (as in ex-Yugoslavia or ex-USSR).[47]

The answer to the question of whether the euro has been a success is less definite and depends on attitudes towards the larger question of European economic integration. The euro was part of an evolutionary process from the European Economic Community centred on customs union to deeper integration that included establishment of the single market. The UK's opt-out from monetary union in the Maastricht Treaty reflected uneasy commitment to ever-closer political union and foreshadowed the Brexit debate of the following quarter century. Denmark's opt-out has been more cosmetic as the krone shadows the euro, although, as with Sweden's de facto opt-out, it reflects a certain lack of commitment to deeper integration. The question for the future concerns the position of the Eastern European EU members who have not joined ERM II, hence showing a lack of interest in adopting the euro and raising the prospect of a two-tier EU consisting of committed integrationists using the common currency and a fringe of less well-integrated member countries who will be absent from a large chunk of economics-related policy negotiations.[48]

---

[47] Eichengreen (2011) agrees that the eurozone was not aligned with OCA criteria, but nevertheless it came into being and future forecasts must accept it as a reality. After arguing that 'Europe's leap to monetary union was a mistake ... compounded by ... including [in the union] also ... Italy, Spain, Portugal and Greece', he goes on to say that 'although a breakup was not impossible ... it was unlikely', given the technical, political and above all economic obstacles. 'On the first minute that word got out that the government was discussing the possibility. Investors would sell their Greek stocks and bonds, for the same reason. This would be a full-fledged financial panic. It would be a full-out bank run. It would be the mother of all financial crises' Eichengreen (2011, 2).

[48] This situation already exists in the composition of the Eurogroup, where the finance ministers of the nineteen eurozone countries meet the day before EU Economic and Financial Affairs Council

Among the nineteen eurozone members, the common currency has consistently had well over 50 per cent support from people participating in Eurobarometer surveys (Roth et al., 2016). Support for the euro fell slightly during the crisis years 2008–13, but quickly recovered to pre-crisis levels. Support for the ECB fell much more drastically during the crisis years 2008–13 and, as of the end of 2019, had not recovered to its pre-crisis level (Roth et al., 2019). This is a better guide to public attitudes in the nineteen eurozone countries than scare stories in the media, especially the anglophone media which reflect the fringe non-euro-using EU members (or ex-member) or thinking in non-member countries. Public satisfaction, especially when serious thinking is required rather than just finding a scapegoat for society's ills, may explain why euro-sceptical populist parties in Greece or Italy backed off from implementing euro-exit once in power.

(ECOFIN) meetings to discuss euro-related business such as the Stability and Growth Pact. A president of the Eurogroup is elected for a renewable two-year term (Jean-Claude Juncker 2005–13, Jeroen Dijsselbloem 2013–17, and Mário Centeno since 2018).

Abbreviations

CAP	common agricultural policy
ECB	European Central Bank
ECOFIN	EU Economic and Financial Affairs Council
ECU	European currency unit (or ecu)
EEC	European Economic Community
EFC	Economic and Financial Committee (preparatory body for ECOFIN)
EMS	European Monetary System
EMU	economic and monetary union
ERM	exchange rate mechanism of the EMS
ESCB	European System of Central Banks
ESM	European Stability Mechanism
ESMA	European Securities and Market Authority
EU	European Union
EWG	Eurogroup Working Group (preparatory body of the Eurogroup)
FDI	foreign direct investment
GATT	General Agreement on Tariffs and Trade (precursor of WTO)
GDP	gross domestic product
GVC	global value chain
IMF	International Monetary Fund
MCA	monetary compensation amount (associated with CAP)
NAFTA	North American Free Trade Agreement (Canada, Mexico & USA)
OCA	optimum currency area
OECD	Organisation for Economic Co-operation and Development
PIIGS	Portugal, Italy, Ireland, Greece and Spain
SBBS	Sovereign Bond-Backed Securities
SEA	Single European Act (1987)
SGP	Stability and Growth Pact (adopted in 1997)
TFEU	Treaty on the Functioning of the European Union (Lisbon Treaty)
TSCG	Intergovernmental Treaty on Stability, Coordination and Governance in the Economic and Monetary Union
UK	United Kingdom (of Great Britain and Northern Ireland)
USA	United States of America
WTO	World Trade Organization (established 1995)

References

Alesina, Alberto, and Robert Barro (2002): Currency Unions, *Quarterly Journal of Economics 117(2)*, 409–36.

Anderson, James (2011): The Gravity Model, *The Annual Review of Economics* 2011(3), 133–60.

Anderson, James, and Eric van Wincoop (2003): Gravity with Gravitas: A Solution to the Border Puzzle, *American Economic Review* 93(1), 170–92.

Artis, Michael, and Mark Taylor (1994): The Stabilizing Effect of the ERM on Exchange Rates and Interest Rates, *IMF Staff Papers 41(1)*, 123–48.

Baldwin, Richard (2016): *The Great Convergence* (Harvard University Press: Cambridge MA).

Baldwin, Richard, and Daria Taglioni (2006): Gravity for Dummies and Dummies for Gravity Equations, *NBER Working Paper No. 12,516*, September.

Basevi, Giorgio, and Silvia Grassi (1993): The Crisis of the European Monetary System and its Consequences for Agricultural Trade. *Review of Economic Conditions in Italy*, June, 81–104.

Bonefeld, Werner, and Peter Burnham (1996): Britain and the Politics of the European Exchange Rate Mechanism 1990–1992, *Capital and Class 20 (3)*, 5–38.

Bozo, Frédéric (2005): *Mitterrand, la fin de la guerre froide et l'unification allemande De Yalta à Maastricht* (Odile Jacob: Paris) – translated as *Mitterrand, the End of the Cold War, and German Unification* (Berghahn Books: New York, 2009).

Braun, Benjamin, and Marina Hübner (2019): *Vanishing Act: The Eurogroup's Accountability* (Transparency International: Brussels).

Brunnermeier, Markus, Harold James and Jean-Pierre Landau (2016): *The Euro and the Battle of Ideas* (Princeton University Press: Princeton NJ).

Commission of the European Communities (1990): One Market, One Money, *European Economy 44*, October.

Cruces, Juan, and Christoph Trebesch (2013): Sovereign Defaults: The Price of Haircuts, *American Economic Journal: Macroeconomics*, 5(3), 85–117.

De Grauwe, Paul (1994): Towards European Monetary Union without the EMS, *Economic Policy 18*, 149–85.

De Grauwe, Paul (2020): *The Economics of Monetary Union*, 13th ed. (Oxford University Press: Oxford, UK).

Eichengreen, Barry (1990): One Money for Europe? Lessons from the U.S. Currency and Customs Union, *Economic Policy 10, April,* 117–87.

Eichengreen, Barry (1993): European Monetary Unification, *Journal of Economic Literature 31(3)*, 1321–57.

Eichengreen, Barry (2011): *Can the Euro Area Hit the Rewind Button?* Unpublished paper, University of California, Berkeley. https://eml .berkeley.edu//~eichengr/can_euro_area_7-23-11.pdf

Eichengreen, Barry (2014): The Eurozzone Crisis: The Theory of Optimum Currency Areas Bites Back, *Notenstein Academy White Paper.* http://citeseerx .ist.psu.edu/viewdoc/download?doi=10.1.1.669.5131&rep=rep1&type=pdf

Eichengreen, Barry (2019): The Euro after Meseberg, *Review of World Economics (Weltwirtschaftliches Archiv) 155(1)*, 15–22.

Farhi, Emmanuel, and Jean Tirole (2018): Deadly Embrace: Sovereign and Financial Balance Sheets Doom Loops, *The Review of Economic Studies 85(3)*, 1781–823

Feldstein, Martin (1992): Europe's Monetary Union: The Case against EMU, *The Economist* (London), 13 June.

Fitzsimmons, Emla, Vincent Hogan and J. Peter Neary (1999): Explaining the Volume of North-South Trade in Ireland: A Gravity Model Approach, *Economic and Social Review 30(4)*, 381–401.

Frankel, Jeffrey (2010): The Estimated Trade Effects of the Euro: Why Are They Below Those from Historical Monetary Unions among Smaller Countries? in Alberto Alesina and Francesco Giavazzi, eds., *Europe and the Euro* (University of Chicago Press for the National Bureau of Economic Research), 169–212.

Frankel, Jeffrey, and Andrew Rose (1998): The Endogeneity of the Optimum Currency Area Criteria, *Economic Journal 108*, 1009–25.

Glick, Reuven (2017): Currency Unions and Regional Trade Agreements: EMU and EU effects on trade, *Comparative Economic Studies 59(2)*, 194–209.

Glick, Reuven, and Andrew Rose (2002): Does a Currency Union Affect Trade? The Time-Series Evidence, *European Economic Review 46(6)*, 1125–51.

Glick, Reuven, and Andrew Rose (2016): Currency Unions and Trade: A post-EMU assessment, *European Economic Review 87*, 78–91.

Grech, John (1978): *Threads of Dependence* (University of Malta Press: Msida, Malta).

Gros, Daniel (2012): The Treaty on Stability, Coordination and Governance in the Economic and Monetary Union (aka Fiscal Compact), CEPS Policy Brief, Centre for European Policy Studies, Brussels.

Gros, Daniel, and Niels Thygesen (1990): The Institutional Approach to Monetary Union in Europe, *Economic Journal 100*, September, 925–35.

Head, Keith, and Thierry Mayer (2015): Gravity Equations: Workhorse, Toolkit, and Cookbook, in Elhanan Helpman, Kenneth Rogoff and Gita Gopinath, eds., *Handbook of International Economics*, vol. 4 (Amsterdam: North-Holland), 131–95.

Howarth, David (2001): *The French Road to the European Monetary Union* (Palgrave: Basingstoke, UK).

Hu, Michael, Christine Jiang and Christos Tsoukalas (2004): The Volatility Impact of the European Monetary System on Member and Non-member Currencies, *Applied Financial Economics 14*, 313–25.

Johnson, Robert and Guillermo Noguera (2012): Proximity and Production Fragmentation, *American Economic Review 102*(3), 407–11.

Johnson, Robert and Guillermo Noguera (2017): A Portrait of Trade in Value-Added over Four Decades, *Review of Economics and Statistics 99* (5), 896–911.

Jonung, Lars, and Eoin Drea (2009): The Euro: It Can't Happen, It's a Bad Idea, It Won't Last. US Economists on the EMU, 1989 – 2002, European Economy Economic Papers 395, European Commission, Brussels.

Kenen, Peter (1969): The Theory of Optimum Currency Areas: An Eclectic View, in Robert Mundell and Alexander Swoboda, eds., *Monetary Problems of the International Economy* (University of Chicago Press: Chicago), 41–60.

Kenen, Peter (2002): Currency Unions and Policy Domains, in David Andrews, C. Randall Henning and Louis Pauly, eds., *Governing the World's Money* (Cornell University Press: Ithaca, NY), 79–104.

Kreinin, Mordechai, and H. Robert Heller (1974): Adjustment Costs, Optimal Currency Areas, and International Reserves, in Willy Sellekaerts (ed.), *International Trade and Finance: Essays in Honour of Jan Tinbergen* (Macmillan: London), 127–40.

Krugman, Paul (1993): What Do We need to Know about the International Monetary System? *Essays in International Economics No.190* (International Economics Section, Princeton University NJ), July.

Krugman, Paul (2013): Revenge of the Optimum Currency Area, in Daron Acemoglu, Jonathan Parker and Michael Woodford, eds., *NBER Macroeconomics Annual 2012*, vol. 27 (University of Chicago Press: Chicago), 439–48.

Lalinsky, Tibor, and Jaanika Meriküll (2019): The Effect of the Single Currency on Exports: Comparative firm-level evidence, *NBS Working Paper 1/2019*, Národná Banka Slovenska, Bratislava.

Lim, Darren, Michalis Moutselos and Michael McKenna (2019): Puzzled Out? The Unsurprising Outcomes of the Greek Bailout Negotiations, *Journal of European Public Policy 26*(3), 325–43.

McCallum, John (1995): National Borders Matter: Canada–US Regional Trade Patterns, *American Economic Review* 85(3), 615–23.

McKinnon, Ronald (1963): Optimum Currency Areas, *American Economic Review 53*, 717–25.

Mayer, Thomas (2012): *Europe's Unfinished Currency: The Political Economics of the Euro* (Anthem Press: London and New York).

Mody, Ashoka (2018): *EuroTragedy: A Drama in Nine Acts* (Oxford University Press).

Mundell, Robert (1961): Theory of Optimum Currency Areas, *American Economic Review 51*, 657–65.

Nguyen, Hoang Sang, and Fabien Rondeau (2019): The Transmission of Business Cycles: Lessons from the 2004 Enlargement of the EU and the Adoption of the Euro, *Economics of Transition and Institutional Change 27 (3)*, 729–43.

Nitsch, Volker (2002): Honey, I Shrunk the Currency Union Effect on Trade, *World Economy 25(4)*, 457–74.

Nitsch, Volker (2003): Have a Break, Have a . . . National Currency: When Do Monetary Unions Fall Apart? Paper presented at the Workshop on Monetary Unions after EMU at the CESifo Venice Summer Institute, 21–22 July 2003.

Nitsch, Volker (2004): Comparing Apples and Oranges: The Effect of Multilateral Currency Unions on Trade is Small, in Volbert Alexander, George von Furstenberg, and Jacques Mélitz eds., *Monetary Unions and Hard Pegs: Effects on Trade, Financial Development, and Stability* (Oxford University Press), 89–100.

Persson, Torsten (2001): Currency Unions and Trade: How Large is the Trade Effect? *Economic Policy*, October, 433–62.

Pomfret, Richard (1991): The Secret of the EMS's Longevity, *Journal of Common Market Studies 29*, 623–33.

Pomfret, Richard (2005): Currency Areas in Theory and Practice, *Economic Record*, 81 (253), 166–76

Pomfret, Richard (2011): *The Age of Equality: The Twentieth Century in Economic Perspective* (Harvard University Press: Cambridge, MA).

Pomfret, Richard (2016): Currency Union and Disunion in Europe and the Former Soviet Union, *CESifo Forum 17(4)*, 43–7.

Pomfret, Richard (forthcoming): *The Economics of European Integration* (Harvard University Press: Cambridge, MA).

Pomfret, Richard, and Patricia Sourdin (2018): Value Chains in Europe and Asia: Which Countries Participate? *International Economics 153*, 34–41.

Roos, Jerome (2019): *Why not Default? The Political Economy of Sovereign Debt* (Princeton University Press: Princeton, NJ).

Rose, Andrew (2000): One Money, One Market: Estimating the Effects of Common Currencies on Trade, *Economic Policy 30*, 9–45.

Rose, Andrew (2002): Honey, the Currency Union Effect on Trade Hasn't Blown Up, *World Economy 25* (*4*), April, 475–9.

Roth, Felix, Edgar Baake, Lars Jonung and Felicitas Nowak-Lehmann (2019): Revisiting Public Support for the Euro, 1999–2017: Accounting for the Crisis and the Recovery, *Journal of Common Market Studies 57*, 1262–73 – summary posted 13 December 2019 as Felix Roth and Lars Jonung: Public Support for the Euro and Trust in the ECB: The First Two Decades. https://voxeu.org/article/public-support-euro-and-trust-ecb.

Roth, Felix, Lars Jonung and Felicitas Nowak-Lehmann (2016): Crisis and Public Support for the Euro, 1990–2014, *Journal of Common Market Studies 54(4)*, 944–60.

Stiglitz, Joseph (2016): *The Euro: How a Common Currency Threatens the Future of Europe* (W.W. Norton: New York).

Thom, Rodney, and Brendan Walsh (2002): The Effect of a Currency Union on Trade: Lessons from the Irish Experience, *European Economic Review 46(6)*, 1111–23.

Tower, Edward, and Thomas Willett (1976): The Theory of Optimum Currency Areas and Exchange-Rate Flexibility, *Princeton Special Papers in International* Economics, *No.11* (International Finance Section, Princeton University), May.

Trebesch, Christoph, and Michael Zabel (2017): The Output Costs of Hard and Soft Sovereign Default, European Economic Review 92, 416–32.

Trichet, Jean-Claude (2019): The Euro after Twenty Years is a Historic Success, *Review of World Economics* (*Weltwirtschaftliches Archiv) 155(1)*, 5–14.

UNIDO (2018): *Global Value Chains and Industrial Development: Lesson from China, South-East and South Asia* (United Nations Industrial Development Organization: Vienna).

Werner Report (1970): *Report to the Council and the Commission on the Realisation by Stages of Economic and Monetary Union in the Community*, Luxembourg. https://ec.europa.eu/economy_finance/publications/pages/publication6142_en.pdf

Cambridge Elements ≡

Economics of European Integration

Nauro F. Campos

University College London

Nauro F. Campos is Professor of Economics at University College London and Research Professor at ETH-Zürich. His main fields of interest are political economy and European integration. He has previously taught at CERGE-EI (Prague), California (Fullerton), Newcastle, Brunel, Bonn, Paris 1 Sorbonne and Warwick. He was a visiting Fulbright Fellow at Johns Hopkins (Baltimore), a Robert McNamara Fellow at The World Bank, and a CBS Fellow at Oxford. He is currently a Research Fellow at IZA-Bonn, a Professorial Fellow at UNU-MERIT (Maastricht University), a member of the Scientific Advisory Board of the (Central) Bank of Finland, and a Senior Fellow of the ESRC Peer Review College. He was a visiting scholar at the University of Michigan, ETH, USC, Bonn, UCL, Stockholm, IMF, World Bank, and the European Commission. From 2009 to 2014, he was seconded as Senior Economic Advisor/SRF to the Chief Economist of the UK's Department for International Development. He received his Ph.D. from the University of Southern California (Los Angeles) in 1997, where he was lucky enough to learn about institutions from Jeff Nugent and Jim Robinson and (more than) happy to be Dick Easterlin's RA. He is the editor in chief of Comparative Economic Studies, the journal of the Association for Comparative Economic Studies.

About the Series

This Element series provides authoritative, up-to-date reviews of core topics and recent developments in the field with particular emphasis on structural, policy and political economy issues. State-of-the- art contributions explore topics such as labour mobility, the euro crisis, Brexit, immigration, inequality, international trade, unemployment, climate change policy, and more.

Cambridge Elements ≡

Economics of European Integration

Elements in the Series

The Road to Monetary Union
Richard Pomfret

A full series listing is available at: www.cambridge.org/EEI

Printed in the United States
by Baker & Taylor Publisher Services